THE
EASY
KOREAN
COOKBOOK
FOR
BEGINNERS

Dear readers,

I'm thrilled to share with you this cookbook that will open up the wonderful world of Korean cuisine. Authentic Korean cooking is renowned worldwide for its bold, complex flavors and healthy ingredients.

In the pages of this book, you'll find 50 recipes for the most beloved Korean dishes like the spicy fermented cabbage kimchi, savory bulgogi beef barbecue, tender galbi ribs, and the national dish bibimbap. I've included Korean classics such as dak galbi spicy chicken, japchae sweet potato glass noodles, hearty doenjang jjigae soybean paste stew, refreshing naengmyeon cold noodles and much more.

Each recipe is designed to give you an authentic taste of Korea. I provide step-by-step instructions, handy tips and tricks, and mouthwatering photos to help you recreate restaurant-quality Korean food at home. You'll learn how to balance the five flavors - spicy, salty, sweet, sour and umami - that are the foundation of Korean cooking. I offer substitutions for hard-to-find ingredients so you can adapt recipes to what's available.

With this cookbook, you'll gain confidence working with ingredients like gochujang chili paste, sesame oil, kimchi, Asian pears, garlic, ginger, seaweed, meat marinades, and more. You'll discover the preparation techniques, cooking methods, and signature flavor pairings that make Korean cuisine so cherished around the world.

I hope this cookbook brings the spirit of Korea to your home cooking. Let these recipes open your palate to new tastes and textures. Share the experience of Korean cuisine with family and friends as you cook sumptuous, mouth-watering Korean meals from your own kitchen. Thank you for choosing my cookbook - now let's get cooking!

감사합니다

Table of

Contents

Calories	Servings	Prep Time	Cook Time
30	6	2H	0M

INGREDIENTS:

- 1 medium Napa cabbage (about 2 lbs / 900 g)
- 1/4 cup sea salt
- 4 cups water
- 1 tablespoon grated ginger
- 1 tablespoon grated garlic
- 1 tablespoon sugar
- 3 tablespoons fish sauce (or soy sauce for a vegan version)
- 3 tablespoons Korean red pepper flakes (Gochugaru)
- 2-3 green onions, chopped
- 1 small carrot, julienned (optional)
- 1 daikon radish, julienned (optional)

DIRECTIONS:

1. Cut the Napa cabbage in half lengthwise and then into bite-sized pieces. Place them in a large mixing bowl.

2. Dissolve the sea salt in water, and pour the saltwater over the cabbage. Make sure the cabbage is fully submerged. Cover with a plate and let it sit for 1-2 hours, tossing it occasionally to ensure even salting.

3. Rinse the salted cabbage thoroughly under cold running water. Squeeze out any excess water and set it aside.

4. In a separate bowl, combine the grated ginger, grated garlic, sugar, fish sauce (or soy sauce), and Korean red pepper flakes to make a paste.

5. Add the paste to the cabbage and mix everything together, wearing disposable gloves if you're sensitive to spicy ingredients.

6. Add the chopped green onions and julienned carrot and daikon radish (if using) to the mixture. Mix well.

7. Pack the kimchi into a clean, airtight container, pressing it down to minimize air pockets. Leave some space at the top as the kimchi will expand during fermentation.

8. Seal the container and let it ferment at room temperature for 1-2 days. After the initial fermentation, store it in the refrigerator for up to a few weeks or longer. The longer it ferments, the more tangy and flavorful it becomes.

Calories	Servings	Prep Time	Cook Time
300	4	1H	15M

INGREDIENTS:

- 1 lbs (500 g) thinly sliced beef (ribeye or sirloin)
- 1 medium onion, thinly sliced
- 2-3 green onions, chopped
- 1 small carrot, julienned
- 1/2 small Asian pear, grated
- 4 cloves garlic, minced
- 1 teaspoon grated ginger
- 1/4 cup soy sauce
- 2 tablespoons sugar
- 1 tablespoon honey
- 2 tablespoons mirin (rice wine)
- 2 tablespoons toasted sesame oil
- 1 tablespoon toasted sesame seeds
- Freshly ground black pepper to taste
- Vegetable oil for grilling

DIRECTIONS:

1. In a bowl, combine the grated Asian pear, minced garlic, grated ginger, soy sauce, sugar, honey, mirin, toasted sesame oil, sesame seeds, and black pepper to make the marinade.

2. Add the thinly sliced beef to the marinade, ensuring it's well coated. Cover and refrigerate for at least 30 minutes, or for a more flavorful result, marinate for up to 4 hours.

3. Preheat your grill or a grill pan to medium-high heat. Brush the grates with vegetable oil to prevent sticking.

4. On the hot grill, place the marinated beef slices, along with the sliced onions, and cook for about 2-3 minutes per side, or until they are cooked to your desired level of doneness. Bulgogi cooks quickly, so be careful not to overcook it.

5. While grilling, you can also add the julienned carrots for a quick char, but they should still have a slight crunch.

6. Once the beef is done, remove it from the grill and let it rest for a few minutes.

7. Serve the grilled beef over a bed of steamed rice, garnished with chopped green onions. You can also serve it with lettuce leaves to make ssam (lettuce wraps).

Calories	Servings	Prep Time	Cook Time
350	4	2H	15M

INGREDIENTS:

- 2 lbs (900 g) of beef short ribs (flanken style, about 1/2-inch thick)
- 1 medium onion, thinly sliced
- 3 cloves garlic, minced
- 2 green onions, chopped
- 1/4 cup soy sauce
- 2 tablespoons sugar
- 2 tablespoons mirin (rice wine)
- 1 tablespoon toasted sesame oil
- 1 tablespoon toasted sesame seeds
- Freshly ground black pepper to taste
- Vegetable oil for grilling

DIRECTIONS:

1. In a bowl, combine the minced garlic, soy sauce, sugar, mirin, toasted sesame oil, sesame seeds, and black pepper to create the marinade.

2. Place the beef short ribs in a large, shallow dish and pour the marinade over them. Make sure all the ribs are well coated. Cover and refrigerate for at least 2 hours, or for a more intense flavor, marinate for up to 6 hours, turning the ribs occasionally.

3. Preheat your grill to medium-high heat and brush the grates with vegetable oil to prevent sticking.

4. Remove the marinated short ribs from the refrigerator and let them come to room temperature for about 30 minutes.

5. Grill the short ribs for about 2-3 minutes per side, or until they reach your desired level of doneness. The meat should be slightly caramelized and have grill marks.

6. While grilling, add the sliced onions to the grill and cook them until they become tender and slightly charred.

7. Once the short ribs are done, remove them from the grill and let them rest for a few minutes.

8. Serve the grilled short ribs with the charred onions, garnished with chopped green onions. Enjoy your delicious Galbi!

Calories	Servings	Prep Time	Cook Time
350	4	30M	0M

INGREDIENTS:

- 8 oz (250 g) Korean glass noodles (dangmyeon)
- 4-5 dried shiitake mushrooms
- 1 small carrot, julienned
- 1 small red bell pepper, julienned
- 1 small yellow bell pepper, julienned
- 1 small onion, thinly sliced
- 2 cloves garlic, minced
- 1 bunch spinach, blanched and cut into 2-inch pieces
- 2 tablespoons vegetable oil
- 2 tablespoons soy sauce
- 1 tablespoon sugar
- 1 tablespoon toasted sesame oil
- Toasted sesame seeds for garnish
- Salt and black pepper to taste

DIRECTIONS:

1. Boil the dried shiitake mushrooms in water for about 30 minutes or until they become soft. Remove the stems and slice the caps thinly.

2. Cook the Korean glass noodles (dangmyeon) according to the package instructions. Usually, this involves boiling them for 6-7 minutes. Drain and rinse with cold water. Cut the noodles with scissors into shorter, more manageable lengths.

3. In a large mixing bowl, combine the cooked noodles with 1 tablespoon of soy sauce and 1 tablespoon of toasted sesame oil. Toss to coat the noodles evenly and set them aside.

4. Heat 1 tablespoon of vegetable oil in a large pan or wok over medium heat. Add the minced garlic and sliced onion, and stir-fry until the onion becomes translucent.

5. Add the julienned carrot, red bell pepper, and yellow bell pepper to the pan and stir-fry for 2-3 minutes, or until they begin to soften.

6. Add the sliced shiitake mushrooms and blanched spinach to the pan. Stir-fry for an additional 2-3 minutes until everything is heated through.

7. Add the cooked glass noodles to the pan and stir-fry everything together for another 2-3 minutes. Season with the remaining 1 tablespoon of soy sauce, sugar, salt, and black pepper.

8. Remove the pan from the heat and let the japchae cool slightly.

9. Garnish with toasted sesame seeds and serve your delicious Japchae as a side dish or a main course.

TTEOKBOKKI
SPICY RICE CAKES

Calories	Servings	Prep Time	Cook Time
300	4	10M	30M

INGREDIENTS:

- 1 lb (500 g) of cylinder-shaped rice cakes (tteok)
- 4 cups water
- 4-5 large dried anchovies (optional, for broth)
- 1 6x6-inch piece of dried kelp (optional, for broth)
- 1/2 onion, thinly sliced
- 2 cloves garlic, minced
- 1/2 cup of gochujang (Korean red pepper paste)
- 2 tablespoons sugar
- 1 tablespoon soy sauce
- 1 teaspoon gochugaru (Korean red pepper flakes, adjust to taste)
- 4-5 hard-boiled eggs (optional)
- 2 green onions, chopped
- 1 sheet of roasted seaweed (gim), crushed into flakes
- Vegetable oil for cooking
- Salt to taste

DIRECTIONS:

1. If you are using dried anchovies and kelp to make broth, combine them with 4 cups of water in a pot. Bring it to a boil and let it simmer for 5-10 minutes. Remove the anchovies and kelp, leaving you with a light, flavorful broth.

2. In a separate bowl, combine the gochujang, sugar, soy sauce, and gochugaru to make the spicy sauce.

3. Heat a large pan or wok over medium heat with a little vegetable oil. Add the sliced onions and minced garlic, and stir-fry for a few minutes until they become fragrant and the onions turn translucent.

4. Add the rice cakes to the pan and pour in the spicy sauce. Stir-fry the rice cakes to coat them evenly with the sauce.

5. Pour in the broth (or plain water if you're not using anchovy and kelp broth), enough to almost cover the rice cakes. Bring it to a boil, then reduce the heat to a simmer.

6. Let the tteokbokki simmer for about 20-25 minutes or until the rice cakes become soft and the sauce thickens. Stir occasionally to prevent sticking.

7. If you're adding hard-boiled eggs, gently add them to the simmering tteokbokki a few minutes before it's done cooking.

8. Taste the sauce and adjust the seasoning with salt or sugar if needed.

9. Just before serving, add the chopped green onions and crushed roasted seaweed flakes as a garnish.

10. Serve your Tteokbokki hot, either as a snack or a meal. Enjoy the spicy, chewy rice cakes!

Calories	Servings	Prep Time	Cook Time
300	4	1H	20M

INGREDIENTS:

- 1 lb (500 g) of thinly sliced pork belly
- 4 cloves garlic, minced
- 1 small onion, thinly sliced
- 4-5 green leaf lettuce leaves
- 4-5 perilla leaves (optional)
- 1/2 small carrot, julienned
- 1 small cucumber, julienned
- 1 small jalapeño pepper, thinly sliced (optional)
- 1/4 cup ssamjang (spicy dipping sauce)
- 1/4 cup doenjang (soybean paste)
- 1/4 cup gochugaru (Korean red pepper flakes)
- 1/4 cup sesame oil
- 1/4 cup soy sauce
- 2 tablespoons sugar
- 2 tablespoons mirin (rice wine)
- Vegetable oil for grilling

DIRECTIONS:

1. In a bowl, combine the minced garlic, soy sauce, sugar, mirin, and sesame oil to create a marinade.

2. Place the thinly sliced pork belly in a shallow dish and pour the marinade over it. Make sure all the pork slices are well coated. Cover and refrigerate for at least 1 hour to marinate.

3. Heat a grill or grill pan over medium-high heat. Brush the grates with vegetable oil to prevent sticking.

4. Once the grill is hot, add the marinated pork belly slices and grill for about 1-2 minutes on each side, or until they're cooked to your preferred level of doneness. Pork belly cooks quickly, so keep an eye on it.

5. While grilling, you can also grill the sliced onions, carrot, and jalapeño pepper for extra flavor.

6. To serve, place a cooked pork belly slice on a lettuce or perilla leaf, add grilled onions, carrot, and jalapeño if desired, and top with a dollop of ssamjang. Wrap it up and enjoy your Samgyeopsal!

7. On the side, serve julienned cucumber for a refreshing crunch and doenjang (soybean paste) mixed with gochugaru for additional dipping.

Calories	Servings	Prep Time	Cook Time
350	4	15M	15M

INGREDIENTS:

- 3 cups cooked and cooled rice
- 1 cup napa cabbage kimchi, chopped
- 1/2 cup kimchi juice
- 2 tablespoons vegetable oil
- 1/2 onion, finely chopped
- 1/2 carrot, finely chopped
- 2 cloves garlic, minced
- 1 cup cooked protein of your choice (e.g., diced chicken, pork, or tofu)
- 2 tablespoons soy sauce
- 1 tablespoon gochugaru (Korean red pepper flakes)
- 1 tablespoon sesame oil
- 2 green onions, chopped
- Toasted sesame seeds for garnish

DIRECTIONS:

1. In a large skillet or wok, heat the vegetable oil over medium-high heat.

2. Add the finely chopped onion and carrot to the skillet and stir-fry for about 2-3 minutes, or until they start to soften.

3. Add the minced garlic and your choice of cooked protein to the skillet. Stir-fry for an additional 2-3 minutes until the protein is heated through.

4. Add the chopped napa cabbage kimchi and continue stir-frying for 2-3 minutes until it's slightly cooked.

5. Push the cooked ingredients to one side of the skillet and add a bit more oil to the empty side. Pour the cooked and cooled rice onto the oiled side of the skillet.

6. Mix the rice with the rest of the ingredients in the skillet and stir-fry for a few minutes, breaking up any clumps and ensuring the rice is well-coated.

7. Pour in the kimchi juice, soy sauce, and gochugaru (Korean red pepper flakes). Continue stir-frying for an additional 3-4 minutes.

8. Drizzle sesame oil over the kimchi fried rice and stir to combine.

9. Add the chopped green onions and stir-fry for another minute or two.

10. Serve your Kimchi Fried Rice hot, garnished with toasted sesame seeds.

Calories	Servings	Prep Time	Cook Time
350	4	30M	30M

INGREDIENTS:

- 1 lb (500 g) boneless chicken thigh, cut into bite-sized pieces
- 2 cups of sliced cabbage
- 1 small sweet potato, thinly sliced
- 1 small onion, thinly sliced
- 1/2 cup scallions, chopped
- 1/2 cup tteok (Korean rice cakes)
- 1/2 cup gochujang (Korean red pepper paste)
- 2 tablespoons soy sauce
- 2 tablespoons sugar
- 2 cloves garlic, minced
- 1 tablespoon grated ginger
- 1 tablespoon cooking oil
- 1 tablespoon sesame oil
- 1 teaspoon gochugaru (Korean red pepper flakes, optional for extra heat)
- Sesame seeds for garnish
- Shredded cheese (optional)
- Vegetable oil for cooking

DIRECTIONS:

1. In a bowl, combine gochujang, soy sauce, sugar, minced garlic, grated ginger, and gochugaru (if using). This will be your spicy sauce.

2. Heat a large skillet or wok over medium-high heat with vegetable oil. Add the chicken pieces and stir-fry until they are cooked through, about 5-7 minutes. Remove the chicken from the skillet and set it aside.

3. In the same skillet, add a bit more vegetable oil if needed. Add the sliced sweet potato and stir-fry for about 5 minutes until they start to soften.

4. Add the sliced onion and continue stir-frying for an additional 2-3 minutes.

5. Add the sliced cabbage, scallions, and tteok (rice cakes) to the skillet. Stir-fry for 2-3 minutes until the vegetables and rice cakes start to cook.

6. Return the cooked chicken to the skillet and pour the spicy sauce over the ingredients.

7. Stir-fry everything together, ensuring the chicken and vegetables are well coated with the sauce, for another 5-7 minutes or until everything is heated through.

8. If you like, you can top the Dak Galbi with shredded cheese and cook for an additional 2-3 minutes until it melts and becomes slightly golden.

9. Just before serving, drizzle with sesame oil and garnish with sesame seeds.

10. Serve your delicious Dak Galbi hot, straight from the skillet.

KIMCHI JJIGAE
KIMCHI STEW

Calories	Servings	Prep Time	Cook Time
250	4	10M	30M

INGREDIENTS:

- 2 cups well-fermented kimchi, chopped
- 1/2 lbs (200-250 g) pork belly or pork shoulder, thinly sliced
- 1 small onion, thinly sliced
- 2 cloves garlic, minced
- 1 small tofu, cubed
- 1 teaspoon gochugaru (Korean red pepper flakes, adjust to taste)
- 1 tablespoon gochujang (Korean red pepper paste)
- 4 cups water
- 1 tablespoon sesame oil
- 2 green onions, chopped
- Salt and pepper to taste

DIRECTIONS:

1. In a large pot, heat sesame oil over medium heat. Add the thinly sliced pork and cook until it starts to brown.

2. Add the minced garlic and gochugaru (Korean red pepper flakes) to the pot. Stir-fry for a minute to release the flavors.

3. Add the chopped kimchi and continue stir-frying for another 5 minutes, allowing the kimchi to become tender and aromatic.

4. Stir in the gochujang (Korean red pepper paste) and continue cooking for 2-3 minutes to enhance the flavor.

5. Add the sliced onion and cook for an additional 2-3 minutes until it becomes translucent.

6. Pour in the water, bring the mixture to a boil, then reduce the heat to a simmer. Cover and let it cook for 15-20 minutes, allowing the flavors to meld together.

7. Add the cubed tofu to the pot and gently stir.

8. Season the stew with salt and pepper to taste.

9. Just before serving, garnish the Kimchi Jjigae with chopped green onions.

10. Serve hot, ideally with a bowl of steamed rice.

Calories	Servings	Prep Time	Cook Time
250	2	10M	20M

INGREDIENTS:

- 1/2 cup minced beef or pork (optional)
- 1/2 onion, finely chopped
- 2 cloves garlic, minced
- 1 small zucchini, thinly sliced
- 1/4 cup kimchi, chopped (optional for extra flavor)
- 2 cups anchovy or vegetable broth
- 1 tube (approximately 14 oz / 400 g) of soft tofu (soondubu)
- 1 egg (optional)
- 1-2 green onions, chopped
- 1 tablespoon gochugaru (Korean red pepper flakes, adjust to taste)
- 1 tablespoon soy sauce
- Salt and pepper to taste
- Sesame oil for garnish

DIRECTIONS:

1. If using meat, heat a small amount of sesame oil in a pot over medium-high heat. Add the minced meat and cook until browned. Remove any excess fat.

2. Add the chopped onion and garlic to the pot, and sauté for 2-3 minutes until they become fragrant and translucent.

3. If you'd like to add kimchi for extra flavor, include it in the pot and stir-fry for another 2-3 minutes.

4. Pour in the anchovy or vegetable broth and bring it to a simmer. Let it cook for about 5-7 minutes to develop the flavors.

5. While the broth simmers, cut the soft tofu into small cubes and add it to the pot. Gently stir to avoid breaking the tofu into smaller pieces.

6. In a separate small bowl, mix the gochugaru (Korean red pepper flakes) with soy sauce to create a paste. Stir this paste into the stew for added flavor and heat.

7. If you'd like to include an egg, crack it into the stew and let it poach in the simmering broth.

8. Season the stew with salt and pepper to taste. If you're using kimchi, you might not need much additional salt.

9. Just before serving, garnish with chopped green onions and a drizzle of sesame oil.

10. Serve your Soondubu Jjigae hot, ideally with a bowl of steamed rice.

Calories	Servings	Prep Time	Cook Time
200	4	20M	20M

INGREDIENTS:

- 1 cup all-purpose flour
- 1 cup water
- 1 egg
- 1 teaspoon soy sauce
- 1 teaspoon salt
- 1/2 teaspoon sugar
- 1/2 teaspoon gochugaru (Korean red pepper flakes, adjust to taste)
- 1 cup mixed seafood (shrimp, squid, and/or mussels), chopped
- 2 cups Korean chives (buchu), chopped into 2-inch pieces
- 1/2 small onion, thinly sliced
- Vegetable oil for cooking
- Dipping sauce: soy sauce, rice vinegar, and sesame seeds

DIRECTIONS:

1. In a large mixing bowl, combine the all-purpose flour, water, egg, soy sauce, salt, sugar, and gochugaru (Korean red pepper flakes). Whisk the ingredients until you have a smooth batter.

2. Add the mixed seafood, Korean chives, and sliced onion to the batter. Mix everything together until the seafood and vegetables are well-coated.

3. Heat a non-stick skillet or a pan over medium-high heat. Add a generous amount of vegetable oil to coat the bottom of the pan.

4. Pour a ladleful of the batter mixture into the hot skillet, spreading it out to form a pancake. The thickness is up to your preference, but it's typically about 1/2 inch thick.

5. Cook the pancake for about 3-4 minutes on each side, or until it's golden brown and crispy. You may need to add more oil when flipping the pancake to ensure even browning.

6. Repeat the process to make additional pancakes with the remaining batter and ingredients.

7. While the pancakes are cooking, mix soy sauce, rice vinegar, and sesame seeds to create a simple dipping sauce.

8. Serve the Haemul Pajeon hot, cut into slices, with the dipping sauce on the side.

Calories	Servings	Prep Time	Cook Time
180	4	20M	15M

INGREDIENTS:

- 1 lb (500 g) fresh squid, cleaned and cut into bite-sized pieces
- 1 small onion, thinly sliced
- 2 cloves garlic, minced
- 1 small carrot, julienned
- 1 small red bell pepper, thinly sliced
- 1 small green bell pepper, thinly sliced
- 2-3 green onions, cut into 2-inch pieces
- 2 tablespoons vegetable oil
- 1 tablespoon gochugaru (Korean red pepper flakes, adjust to taste)
- 2 tablespoons soy sauce
- 1 tablespoon sugar
- 1 tablespoon mirin (rice wine)
- 1 tablespoon toasted sesame oil
- Sesame seeds for garnish

DIRECTIONS:

1. In a bowl, mix together the minced garlic, gochugaru (Korean red pepper flakes), soy sauce, sugar, mirin, and toasted sesame oil to create the marinade.

2. In a large skillet or wok, heat the vegetable oil over medium-high heat.

3. Add the sliced onion and julienned carrot to the skillet, and stir-fry for about 2-3 minutes until they start to soften.

4. Add the squid pieces to the skillet and stir-fry for an additional 3-4 minutes until they are partially cooked.

5. Add the red and green bell pepper slices, and continue stir-frying for 2-3 minutes until the vegetables become tender.

6. Pour the marinade over the ingredients in the skillet and mix well to ensure everything is coated evenly.

7. Add the green onions to the skillet and stir-fry for another 2-3 minutes until they are heated through.

8. Taste and adjust the seasoning if needed, adding more gochugaru or sugar according to your preference.

9. Just before serving, garnish the Ojingeo Bokkeum with sesame seeds.

10. Serve hot, typically with a bowl of steamed rice.

DOENJANG JJIGAE
SOYBEAN PASTE STEW

Calories	Servings	Prep Time	Cook Time
150	4	10M	20M

INGREDIENTS:

- 2 tablespoons doenjang (Korean soybean paste)
- 1 small zucchini, sliced
- 1 small potato, peeled and cubed
- 1 small onion, thinly sliced
- 2 cloves garlic, minced
- 1 small green chili pepper, sliced (optional, for extra heat)
- 1 small tofu, cubed
- 4-5 dried shiitake mushrooms, rehydrated and sliced
- 4 cups water or anchovy broth
- 1 tablespoon sesame oil
- 1 tablespoon vegetable oil
- Salt and pepper to taste
- Sliced green onions for garnish

DIRECTIONS:

1. In a pot, heat the vegetable oil over medium heat. Add the minced garlic and sliced onion. Sauté for about 2-3 minutes until they become fragrant and translucent.

2. Add the cubed potato and shiitake mushrooms to the pot. Stir for an additional 3-4 minutes until they begin to cook.

3. Pour in the water or anchovy broth and bring it to a simmer. Let it cook for about 10-15 minutes until the potatoes are tender.

4. While the soup simmers, add the doenjang (Korean soybean paste) to a small bowl and mix it with a few tablespoons of water to create a smooth paste.

5. Add the doenjang paste to the simmering soup and stir well to ensure it's fully dissolved.

6. Add the zucchini, tofu, and green chili pepper (if using) to the pot. Let the stew simmer for an additional 5-7 minutes until the zucchini is tender.

7. Season the Doenjang Jjigae with salt and pepper to taste. Adjust the flavor by adding more soybean paste if needed.

8. Just before serving, drizzle sesame oil over the stew and garnish with sliced green onions.

9. Serve the Doenjang Jjigae hot, typically with a bowl of steamed rice.

Calories	Servings	Prep Time	Cook Time
300	4	30M	2H

INGREDIENTS:

- 2 lbs (1 kg) pork belly, skin on
- 4 cups water
- 1 small onion, roughly chopped
- 1 thumb-sized piece of ginger, sliced
- 4 cloves garlic, crushed
- 2-3 green onions, chopped
- 2 tablespoons soybean paste (doenjang)
- 2 tablespoons sugar
- 2 teaspoons salt
- Freshly ground black pepper
- 1 head of Napa cabbage
- 1 bunch of Korean perilla leaves (kkaennip)
- Ssamjang (spicy dipping sauce)
- Kimchi
- Fresh garlic cloves
- Fresh chili peppers (optional)

DIRECTIONS:

1. In a large pot, bring 4 cups of water to a boil.

2. Add the pork belly, skin side down, into the boiling water. Let it cook for 10-15 minutes to remove impurities and excess fat. Drain and rinse the pork under cold water.

3. Return the pork to the pot, and add the roughly chopped onion, sliced ginger, crushed garlic, and chopped green onions.

4. Fill the pot with enough water to cover the pork. Bring it to a boil, then reduce the heat to low and let it simmer for about 1.5 to 2 hours, or until the pork is tender.

5. While the pork is simmering, prepare the seasoning paste. In a small bowl, mix the soybean paste (doenjang), sugar, salt, and freshly ground black pepper.

6. Remove the cooked pork from the pot, and let it cool slightly. Once it's cool enough to handle, slice it into thin, bite-sized pieces.

7. Prepare the Napa cabbage by cutting it into bite-sized pieces. Rinse the cabbage under cold water and drain it.

8. Wash the Korean perilla leaves (kkaennip) and set them aside.

9. To serve, place the sliced pork, Napa cabbage, perilla leaves, and kimchi on a large platter. Set out the fresh garlic cloves and fresh chili peppers if desired.

10. To make a wrap, take a perilla leaf or a piece of Napa cabbage, add a slice of pork, a dab of ssamjang, and any other desired accompaniments. Wrap it up and enjoy your Bossam!

Calories	Servings	Prep Time	Cook Time
250	2	15M	15M

INGREDIENTS:

- 1 tube (approximately 14 oz / 400 g) of soft tofu (sundubu)
- 1/4 lbs (100 g) of clams or mussels (optional)
- 4-5 large shrimp, peeled and deveined (optional)
- 1 small onion, thinly sliced
- 2 cloves garlic, minced
- 1 small zucchini, thinly sliced
- 1 small carrot, julienned
- 1 small red chili pepper, thinly sliced (adjust to taste)
- 1 small green chili pepper, thinly sliced (adjust to taste)
- 2-3 shiitake mushrooms, sliced
- 2 cups anchovy or vegetable broth
- 2 tablespoons gochugaru (Korean red pepper flakes, adjust to taste)
- 1 tablespoon soy sauce
- 1 tablespoon sesame oil
- Salt and pepper to taste
- Sliced green onions for garnish

DIRECTIONS:

1. In a pot, heat sesame oil over medium heat. Add the minced garlic and sliced onion. Sauté for about 2-3 minutes until they become fragrant and translucent.

2. If you're using clams or mussels, add them to the pot and stir for a few minutes until they start to open.

3. Pour in the anchovy or vegetable broth and bring it to a simmer. Let it cook for about 5-7 minutes to develop the flavors.

4. While the broth simmers, cut the soft tofu into small cubes and add it to the pot. Gently stir to avoid breaking the tofu into smaller pieces.

5. Add the sliced zucchini, carrot, shiitake mushrooms, and chili peppers to the pot. Let the stew simmer for an additional 5-7 minutes until the vegetables are tender.

6. In a small bowl, mix the gochugaru (Korean red pepper flakes) with soy sauce to create a paste. Stir this paste into the stew for added flavor and heat.

7. If you're using shrimp, add them to the stew and let them cook for a few minutes until they turn pink.

8. Season the Sundubu Jjigae with salt and pepper to taste. Adjust the spiciness by adding more gochugaru if needed.

9. Just before serving, garnish with sliced green onions.

10. Serve the spicy tofu stew hot, ideally with a bowl of steamed rice.

Calories	Servings	Prep Time	Cook Time
300	4	20M	10M

INGREDIENTS:

- 14 oz (400 g) of naengmyeon noodles (Korean cold noodles)
- 1 small cucumber, julienned
- 2 boiled eggs, sliced
- 1 small pear, julienned
- 1 small apple, julienned
- 1/2 small red bell pepper, thinly sliced
- 1/2 small yellow bell pepper, thinly sliced
- 2 tablespoons toasted sesame seeds
- 4-6 ice cubes

For the Bibim Naengmyeon Sauce:

- 2 tablespoo ns gochugaru (Korean red pepper flakes)
- 2 tablespoons gochujang (Korean red pepper paste)
- 2 tablespoons sugar
- 2 tablespoons soy sauce
- 2 tablespoons rice vinegar
- 2 cloves garlic, minced
- 1 tablespoon toasted sesame oil
- 1 tablespoon vegetable oil

DIRECTIONS:

1. Cook the naengmyeon noodles according to the package instructions. They are typically boiled for 3-4 minutes. Drain and rinse the noodles under cold running water to cool them down.

2. In a large mixing bowl, combine all the ingredients for the Bibim Naengmyeon Sauce: gochugaru, gochujang, sugar, soy sauce, rice vinegar, minced garlic, toasted sesame oil, and vegetable oil. Mix well until it forms a smooth sauce.

3. In the same mixing bowl, add the cooled naengmyeon noodles to the sauce. Toss the noodles until they are well-coated with the sauce.

4. To serve, place the spicy noodles in individual serving bowls. Top them with julienned cucumber, pear, apple, boiled egg slices, and sliced bell peppers.

5. Sprinkle toasted sesame seeds over the noodles and add ice cubes to each bowl to keep the dish extra cold.

6. Serve your Bibim Naengmyeon immediately, and mix everything together before eating for a delicious and refreshing cold noodle dish.

Calories	Servings	Prep Time	Cook Time
100	4	15M	15M

INGREDIENTS:

- 2 medium zucchinis
- 1 small onion
- 1/2 cup all-purpose flour
- 2 tablespoons water
- 1 egg
- 1/2 teaspoon salt
- Vegetable oil for frying
- Soy sauce and vinegar for dipping (optional)

DIRECTIONS:

1. Grate the zucchinis and the onion using a grater or food processor.

2. Place the grated zucchini and onion in a clean kitchen towel or cheesecloth. Squeeze out the excess liquid.

3. In a mixing bowl, combine the squeezed zucchini and onion with all-purpose flour, water, egg, and salt. Mix well until the ingredients form a batter.

4. Heat vegetable oil in a non-stick skillet or frying pan over medium-high heat.

5. Spoon a portion of the zucchini batter into the skillet, spreading it out to form a pancake. The thickness can vary depending on your preference.

6. Cook the pancake for about 2-3 minutes on each side, or until it becomes golden brown and crispy. You may need to add more oil when flipping the pancake to ensure even browning.

7. Remove the cooked zucchini pancake from the skillet and place it on a plate lined with paper towels to remove excess oil.

8. Repeat the process with the remaining batter to make additional pancakes.

9. Serve your Hobak Jeon hot, typically with a dipping sauce made from soy sauce and vinegar if desired.

Calories	Servings	Prep Time	Cook Time
350	4	30M	2H

INGREDIENTS:

- 2 lbs (900 g) pork neck bones or spine, cut into sections
- 1 small onion, quartered
- 1 small potato, peeled and cubed
- 4-5 cloves garlic, minced
- 1 small zucchini, sliced
- 1 small carrot, sliced
- 1 small onion, thinly sliced
- 1 small green chili pepper, sliced (adjust to taste)
- 2-3 green onions, chopped
- 2 tablespoons gochugaru (Korean red pepper flakes, adjust to taste)
- 1 tablespoon soy sauce
- 1 tablespoon doenjang (Korean soybean paste)
- 1 tablespoon sesame oil
- Salt and pepper to taste

DIRECTIONS:

1. In a large pot, bring water to a boil. Add the pork neck bones or spine sections and boil for about 5-10 minutes to remove impurities and excess fat. Drain and rinse the bones under cold water.

2. In a clean pot, place the parboiled pork bones and cover them with water. Bring it to a boil, then reduce the heat to a simmer. Let it cook for about 1.5 to 2 hours, occasionally skimming off any foam or impurities that rise to the surface.

3. Add the quartered onion, minced garlic, and potato to the pot. Continue simmering for an additional 30 minutes, or until the pork and potatoes become tender.

4. Add the zucchini, carrot, sliced onion, and green chili pepper to the pot. Let it simmer for another 10-15 minutes until the vegetables are tender.

5. In a separate small bowl, mix the gochugaru (Korean red pepper flakes), soy sauce, and doenjang (Korean soybean paste) with a bit of water to create a smooth paste.

6. Add this paste to the soup and stir well to ensure it's fully dissolved.

7. Season the Gamjatang with salt and pepper to taste. Adjust the level of spiciness by adding more gochugaru according to your preference.

8. Just before serving, garnish the soup with chopped green onions and a drizzle of sesame oil.

9. Serve your Gamjatang hot, typically with a bowl of steamed rice.

Calories	Servings	Prep Time	Cook Time
300	4	20M	1H30M

INGREDIENTS:

- 8 cups water
- 1/2 lbs (250 g) beef (brisket or shank), thinly sliced
- 1 small onion, thinly sliced
- 1 small carrot, julienned
- 1 small zucchini, julienned
- 4-5 cloves garlic, minced
- 2 green onions, chopped
- 1/2 cup fernbrake (gosari), soaked and cut into bite-sized pieces
- 1/2 cup soaked and sliced mu (Korean radish)
- 4-5 dried shiitake mushrooms, rehydrated and sliced
- 1/2 cup soaked and sliced daseulgi (fernbrake stems)
- 2 eggs, beaten
- 3 tablespoons gochugaru (Korean red pepper flakes, adjust to taste)
- 2 tablespoons soy sauce
- 2 tablespoons sesame oil
- Salt and pepper to taste

DIRECTIONS:

1. In a large pot, bring 8 cups of water to a boil.

2. Add the thinly sliced beef and cook for about 5 minutes, or until the meat is no longer pink. Remove any excess foam or impurities that rise to the surface.

3. Add the sliced onion, julienned carrot, zucchini, minced garlic, and green onions to the pot. Let it simmer for about 10-15 minutes, or until the vegetables become tender.

4. Add the soaked and prepared fernbrake (gosari), mu (Korean radish), shiitake mushrooms, and daseulgi (fernbrake stems) to the soup. Continue to simmer for an additional 15-20 minutes.

5. In a separate bowl, mix the gochugaru (Korean red pepper flakes), soy sauce, and sesame oil to create a paste. Stir this paste into the soup for added flavor and heat.

6. Season the Yukgaejang with salt and pepper to taste. Adjust the level of spiciness by adding more gochugaru according to your preference.

7. Just before serving, slowly drizzle beaten eggs into the soup while stirring gently. The eggs will cook quickly and create strands in the soup.

8. Serve your Yukgaejang hot, ideally with a bowl of steamed rice.

Calories	Servings	Prep Time	Cook Time
70	4	5M	5M

INGREDIENTS:

- 12 oz (about 2 cups) soybean sprouts (kongnamul)
- 2 cloves garlic, minced
- 2 green onions, chopped
- 1 tablespoon sesame oil
- 1 tablespoon soy sauce
- 1 teaspoon toasted sesame seeds
- 1/2 teaspoon salt
- 1/2 teaspoon sugar
- 1/4 teaspoon gochugaru (Korean red pepper flakes, adjust to taste)

DIRECTIONS:

1. Rinse the soybean sprouts under cold water and drain them.

2. Bring a pot of water to a boil. Add the soybean sprouts to the boiling water and cook for about 3-5 minutes until they become tender but still crisp. Be careful not to overcook them.

3. Drain the cooked soybean sprouts and rinse them under cold water to cool and stop the cooking process. Drain again.

4. In a mixing bowl, combine the soybean sprouts with minced garlic, chopped green onions, sesame oil, soy sauce, toasted sesame seeds, salt, sugar, and gochugaru (Korean red pepper flakes). Mix well to ensure the soybean sprouts are evenly coated with the seasoning.

5. Serve your Kongnamul Muchim cold as a side dish or banchan in a traditional Korean meal.

Calories	Servings	Prep Time	Cook Time
400	4	20M	20M

INGREDIENTS:

- 14 oz (400 g) of Korean jjajangmyeon noodles or Chinese wheat noodles
- 1/2 lb (250 g) pork belly, thinly sliced
- 1 small onion, finely chopped
- 1 small zucchini, diced
- 1 small potato, diced
- 1 small carrot, diced
- 1/2 cup Korean chunjang (black bean paste)
- 2 cups water
- 2 tablespoons vegetable oil
- 1 tablespoon sugar
- Salt and pepper to taste
- Cucumber and radish pickles for garnish (optional)

DIRECTIONS:

1. Cook the jjajangmyeon or Chinese wheat noodles according to the package instructions. Drain and set them aside.

2. In a large skillet or wok, heat vegetable oil over medium-high heat. Add the thinly sliced pork belly and cook until it becomes browned and crispy.

3. Add the finely chopped onion to the skillet and sauté until it becomes translucent.

4. Stir in the diced zucchini, potato, and carrot. Cook for a few minutes until the vegetables start to soften.

5. Add the Korean chunjang (black bean paste) to the skillet and mix it well with the other ingredients.

6. Pour in the water and sugar, and stir until the sauce thickens. Simmer for about 5-7 minutes until the vegetables are tender.

7. Season the black bean sauce with salt and pepper to taste.

8. To serve, place a portion of the cooked noodles in individual bowls and top them with the black bean sauce.

9. Garnish your Jjajangmyeon with cucumber and radish pickles if desired.

10. Enjoy your Black Bean Noodles hot, traditionally served with a side of pickled radish.

Calories	Servings	Prep Time	Cook Time
50	30	45M	15M

INGREDIENTS:

For the Dumpling Filling:

- 1/2 lb (250 g) ground pork
- 1/2 lb (250 g) ground beef
- 1 cup napa cabbage, finely chopped
- 1/2 cup tofu, drained and mashed
- 1/2 cup onion, finely chopped
- 1/4 cup carrot, finely chopped
- 1/4 cup green onions, finely chopped
- 2 cloves garlic, minced
- 1 tablespoon soy sauce
- 1 tablespoon sesame oil
- 1 teaspoon sugar
- 1/2 teaspoon salt
- 1/4 teaspoon black pepper

For Wrapping and Sealing Dumplings:

- 1 package of dumpling wrappers (round or square)
- Water for sealing

For Cooking Dumplings:

- 2 tablespoons vegetable oil
- 1/2 cup water

DIRECTIONS:

1. In a large mixing bowl, combine the ground pork and beef.

2. Add the finely chopped napa cabbage, mashed tofu, chopped onion, carrot, green onions, minced garlic, soy sauce, sesame oil, sugar, salt, and black pepper to the meat mixture.

3. Mix the ingredients well, ensuring that everything is evenly combined.

4. To wrap the dumplings, take a dumpling wrapper and place about 1 tablespoon of the filling in the center.

5. Wet the edges of the wrapper with a little water.

6. Fold the wrapper in half to create a half-moon shape, then press the edges together to seal the dumpling.

7. You can leave the dumplings as half-moon shapes or pleat the edges to create a more decorative look.

8. In a large skillet, heat vegetable oil over medium-high heat.

9. Place the dumplings in the skillet and cook for a few minutes until the bottoms become golden brown.

10. Pour in 1/2 cup of water and cover the skillet with a lid.

11. Let the dumplings steam for about 5-7 minutes, or until the water has evaporated.

12. Continue cooking the dumplings uncovered for an additional 3-5 minutes, allowing them to crisp up.

13. Serve your Mandu hot with a dipping sauce made from soy sauce and vinegar, or your preferred dipping sauce.

Calories	Servings	Prep Time	Cook Time
250	4	30M	0M

INGREDIENTS:

For the Gimbap Rice:
- 2 cups sushi rice (short-grain rice)
- 2 tablespoons rice vinegar
- 1 tablespoon sugar
- 1 teaspoon salt

For the Gimbap Filling:
- 4 sheets of gim (roasted seaweed)
- 1/2 lb (250 g) bulgogi (marinated and grilled beef), sliced into thin strips
- 4 imitation crab sticks, halved lengthwise
- 1 cucumber, julienned
- 2 carrots, julienned and blanched
- 4 eggs, beaten and made into thin omelets
- 1/2 bunch of spinach, blanched and seasoned with soy sauce and sesame oil

For the Gimbap Dipping Sauce:
- 2 tablespoons soy sauce
- 1 tablespoon vinegar
- 1 teaspoon sugar
- 1 teaspoon toasted sesame seeds
- 1 clove garlic, minced
- 1/2 teaspoon gochugaru (Korean red pepper flakes, adjust to taste)

DIRECTIONS:

1. Cook the sushi rice according to the package instructions. While it's still warm, season the rice with rice vinegar, sugar, and salt. Mix well and let it cool to room temperature.

2. Lay out a bamboo sushi rolling mat and cover it with plastic wrap. Place a sheet of roasted seaweed (gim) on the mat.

3. Wet your hands and take a small handful of seasoned rice, then spread it evenly over the seaweed, leaving a small border along the top edge.

4. Lay the bulgogi, imitation crab sticks, cucumber, carrot, egg omelet, and seasoned spinach in a neat row across the center of the rice.

5. Carefully lift the bamboo mat with your thumbs and roll it over the filling while tucking it in firmly. Roll until you reach the exposed edge of the seaweed.

6. Dampen the exposed edge with a little water to help seal the gimbap roll.

7. Once the gimbap is rolled, use the bamboo mat to shape it into a tight cylinder.

8. Slice the gimbap roll into bite-sized pieces with a sharp, wet knife.

9. To make the dipping sauce, combine soy sauce, vinegar, sugar, toasted sesame seeds, minced garlic, and gochugaru (Korean red pepper flakes) in a small bowl. Mix well.

10. Serve your Gimbap with the dipping sauce and enjoy as a delightful Korean snack or meal.

Calories	Servings	Prep Time	Cook Time
250	4	30M	0M

INGREDIENTS:

For the Kimbap Rice:

- 2 cups sushi rice (short-grain rice)
- 2 tablespoons rice vinegar
- 1 tablespoon sugar
- 1 teaspoon salt

For the Kimbap Filling:

- 4 sheets of gim (roasted seaweed)
- 1/2 lb (250 g) bulgogi (marinated and grilled beef), sliced into thin strips
- 4 imitation crab sticks, halved lengthwise
- 1 cucumber, julienned
- 2 carrots, julienned and blanched
- 4 eggs, beaten and made into thin omelets
- 1/2 bunch of spinach, blanched and seasoned with soy sauce and sesame oil

For the Kimbap Dipping Sauce:

- 2 tablespoons soy sauce
- 1 tablespoon vinegar
- 1 teaspoon sugar
- 1 teaspoon toasted sesame seeds
- 1 clove garlic, minced
- 1/2 teaspoon gochugaru (Korean red pepper flakes, adjust to taste)

DIRECTIONS:

1. Cook the sushi rice according to the package instructions. While it's still warm, season the rice with rice vinegar, sugar, and salt. Mix well and let it cool to room temperature.

2. Lay out a bamboo sushi rolling mat and cover it with plastic wrap. Place a sheet of roasted seaweed (gim) on the mat.

3. Wet your hands and take a small handful of seasoned rice, then spread it evenly over the seaweed, leaving a small border along the top edge.

4. Lay the bulgogi, imitation crab sticks, cucumber, carrot, egg omelet, and seasoned spinach in a neat row across the center of the rice.

5. Carefully lift the bamboo mat with your thumbs and roll it over the filling while tucking it in firmly. Roll until you reach the exposed edge of the seaweed.

6. Dampen the exposed edge with a little water to help seal the kimbap roll.

7. Once the kimbap is rolled, use the bamboo mat to shape it into a tight cylinder.

8. Slice the kimbap roll into bite-sized pieces with a sharp, wet knife.

9. To make the dipping sauce, combine soy sauce, vinegar, sugar, toasted sesame seeds, minced garlic, and gochugaru (Korean red pepper flakes) in a small bowl. Mix well.

10. Serve your Kimbap with the dipping sauce and enjoy as a delightful Korean snack or meal.

DRIED SEAWEED SOUP
MIYEOK

Calories	Servings	Prep Time	Cook Time
100	4	30M	30M

INGREDIENTS:

- 1/2 cup dried seaweed (miyeok)
- 8 cups water
- 1 tablespoon sesame oil
- 1 small onion, thinly sliced
- 2 cloves garlic, minced
- 1 medium carrot, julienned
- 1/2 cup sliced shiitake mushrooms
- 2 tablespoons soy sauce
- Salt and pepper to taste
- Chopped green onions (for garnish)

DIRECTIONS:

1. Start by soaking the dried seaweed (miyeok) in a large bowl of water. Allow it to soak for about 30 minutes or until it has expanded and softened.

2. Rinse the soaked seaweed under cold running water and cut it into smaller, bite-sized pieces.

3. In a large pot, heat the sesame oil over medium heat. Add the sliced onion and minced garlic. Sauté for a few minutes until the onion is translucent.

4. Add the julienned carrot and shiitake mushrooms to the pot. Sauté for another 2-3 minutes.

5. Pour in 8 cups of water and bring it to a boil.

6. Add the soaked and cut dried seaweed to the boiling water. Simmer for about 20 minutes or until the seaweed is tender.

7. Season the soup with soy sauce and salt and pepper to taste. Adjust the seasoning according to your preference.

8. Serve the Dried Seaweed (Miyeok) Soup hot, garnished with chopped green onions.

Calories	Servings	Prep Time	Cook Time
500	4	30M	30M

INGREDIENTS:

For the Rice and Vegetables:

- 2 cups cooked short-grain rice
- 2 cups spinach, blanched and seasoned with soy sauce and sesame oil
- 2 cups bean sprouts, blanched and seasoned with soy sauce and sesame oil
- 2 cups julienned carrots, sautéed
- 2 cups julienned zucchini, sautéed
- 2 cups sliced mushrooms, sautéed
- 1 cup sliced shiitake mushrooms, sautéed
- 1 cup sliced bell peppers, sautéed

For the Bibimbap Sauce:

- 4 tablespoons gochujang (Korean red pepper paste)
- 2 tablespoons soy sauce
- 2 tablespoons sugar
- 1 tablespoon sesame oil
- 1 clove garlic, minced

For Assembly and Garnish:

- 4 large dolsot (stone pots)
- 4 fried eggs
- Toasted sesame seeds
- Julienned cucumber
- Sliced nori seaweed

DIRECTIONS:

1. Prepare the rice in a rice cooker or following the package instructions. When it's ready, divide it into four portions and place one portion in each dolsot (stone pot).

2. Arrange the blanched and seasoned spinach, bean sprouts, sautéed carrots, zucchini, mushrooms, and bell peppers in separate sections on top of the rice in each stone pot.

3. In a small bowl, mix together the Bibimbap Sauce ingredients: gochujang, soy sauce, sugar, sesame oil, and minced garlic.

4. Heat the stone pots on a stovetop over medium-high heat. Let them sizzle for about 5-7 minutes until the rice at the bottom becomes crispy and golden brown.

5. Just before serving, top each Bibimbap with a fried egg and garnish with toasted sesame seeds, julienned cucumber, and sliced nori seaweed.

6. Serve your Bibimbap with Dolsot hot, with the Bibimbap Sauce served on the side. Mix the sauce into the ingredients to your taste and enjoy!

Calories	Servings	Prep Time	Cook Time
300	4	1H	15M

INGREDIENTS:

For the Noodles and Broth:

- 14 oz (400 g) of naengmyeon noodles (buckwheat noodles)
- 4 cups beef or vegetable broth
- 2 cups water
- 1/4 cup soy sauce
- 3 tablespoons sugar
- 2 tablespoons rice vinegar
- 1 tablespoon sesame oil
- 1 tablespoon gochugaru (Korean red pepper flakes, adjust to taste)
- 2 cloves garlic, minced
- Ice cubes (for serving)

For Toppings (Customize to Your Preference):

- Thinly sliced cucumber
- Asian pear, julienned
- Hard-boiled eggs, halved
- Radish kimchi (kkakdugi)
- Thinly sliced beef (usually boiled and thinly sliced)
- Sautéed mushrooms
- Thinly sliced scallions
- Sesame seeds

DIRECTIONS:

1. In a large pot, combine beef or vegetable broth, water, soy sauce, sugar, rice vinegar, sesame oil, gochugaru (Korean red pepper flakes), and minced garlic. Bring the mixture to a boil, then reduce the heat and simmer for about 10 minutes. Let the broth cool to room temperature.

2. While the broth is cooling, bring a large pot of water to a boil. Cook the naengmyeon noodles according to the package instructions (usually about 3-4 minutes). Drain the noodles and rinse them under cold running water until they are cool.

3. Serve the cooked naengmyeon noodles in individual serving bowls and top them with the desired toppings. Traditional toppings often include thinly sliced cucumber, Asian pear, hard-boiled eggs, radish kimchi, sliced beef, and scallions.

4. Pour the cooled broth over the noodles. Add a handful of ice cubes to each bowl for an extra refreshing touch.

5. Sprinkle sesame seeds on top and serve your Naengmyeon cold. Enjoy the delicious, chilled buckwheat noodles.

INGREDIENTS:

Calories	Servings	Prep Time	Cook Time
180	4	15M	20M

INGREDIENTS:

- 1 cup all-purpose flour
- 1 cup water
- 1 egg
- 1 teaspoon soy sauce
- 1/2 teaspoon salt
- 1/4 teaspoon black pepper
- 1 cup fresh oysters
- 1/2 cup sliced scallions
- 1/2 cup sliced onion
- Vegetable oil for frying

DIRECTIONS:

1. In a mixing bowl, combine the all-purpose flour, water, egg, soy sauce, salt, and black pepper. Mix until you have a smooth pancake batter.

2. Add the fresh oysters, sliced scallions, and sliced onion to the batter. Gently fold them in, ensuring an even distribution.

3. Heat a non-stick skillet or frying pan over medium-high heat. Add a generous amount of vegetable oil to coat the bottom of the pan.

4. Pour a ladle of the oyster pancake batter into the hot pan, spreading it out to create a thin, even layer.

5. Cook for about 2-3 minutes on each side, or until the pancake is golden brown and crispy.

6. Repeat the process with the remaining batter, adding more oil to the pan as needed.

7. Once all the oyster pancakes are cooked, transfer them to a plate lined with paper towels to remove excess oil.

8. Serve the Guljeon (Oyster Pancake) hot, with a dipping sauce made of soy sauce, vinegar, and a pinch of sugar if desired.

Calories	Servings	Prep Time	Cook Time
300	4	15M	20M

INGREDIENTS:

- 14 oz (400 g) of dduk (Korean rice cakes)
- 1/2 cup of fish cake slices
- 1/2 cup of cabbage, thinly sliced
- 1/2 cup of scallions, chopped into 2-inch pieces
- 1/4 cup of gochugaru (Korean red pepper flakes)
- 2 tablespoons of soy sauce
- 2 tablespoons of sugar
- 2 tablespoons of gochujang (Korean red pepper paste)
- 1 tablespoon of sesame oil
- 1 tablespoon of vegetable oil
- 3 cups of water
- 1 hard-boiled egg (optional)
- Roasted sesame seeds (for garnish)

DIRECTIONS:

1. Soak the dduk (rice cakes) in warm water for about 15 minutes to soften them. Drain and set aside.

2. In a large pan or wok, heat the vegetable oil over medium heat. Add the gochugaru (Korean red pepper flakes) and stir-fry for a minute to release its flavor and aroma.

3. Add the sliced fish cakes and stir-fry for a few minutes until they start to brown.

4. Stir in the thinly sliced cabbage and scallions, and continue to cook for a couple of minutes until they begin to soften.

5. Add the soaked dduk (rice cakes) to the pan and mix well with the other ingredients.

6. In a small bowl, combine the soy sauce, sugar, gochujang (Korean red pepper paste), and sesame oil to make a sauce. Pour the sauce over the ingredients in the pan.

7. Add the water to the pan and bring it to a boil. Reduce the heat and simmer for about 10-15 minutes, or until the dduk (rice cakes) become tender and the sauce thickens.

8. If you'd like, garnish your Ddukbokki with a halved hard-boiled egg and a sprinkle of roasted sesame seeds.

9. Serve your Spicy Rice Cake Stir-Fry hot, as a popular Korean street food dish or snack.

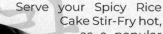

Calories	Servings	Prep Time	Cook Time
80	4	10M	20M

INGREDIENTS:

- 1/2 cup dried miyeok (seaweed)
- 6 cups water
- 1 tablespoon sesame oil
- 1 tablespoon minced garlic
- 1 tablespoon soy sauce
- Salt to taste
- 4 cups beef or vegetable broth
- 1/2 cup sliced beef or tofu
- 2 cups sliced zucchini
- 2 cups sliced green onions
- Cooked rice (optional, for serving)

DIRECTIONS:

1. Start by soaking the dried miyeok (seaweed) in cold water for about 10 minutes, or until it becomes soft and rehydrated. Drain and cut it into bite-sized pieces.

2. In a large pot, heat the sesame oil over medium heat. Add the minced garlic and sauté for a minute until fragrant.

3. Add the soaked and drained miyeok (seaweed) to the pot and stir-fry for a few more minutes.

4. Pour in the water and beef or vegetable broth, then bring the mixture to a boil.

5. Reduce the heat and let the soup simmer for about 15-20 minutes until the seaweed is tender.

6. Season the soup with soy sauce, salt, and pepper to taste.

7. Add the sliced beef or tofu, zucchini, and green onions to the soup. Simmer for an additional 5-7 minutes until the ingredients are fully cooked.

8. Serve your Miyeokguk hot, with or without a side of cooked rice, as a traditional Korean dish often enjoyed on birthdays and for postpartum recovery.

MAEUNTANG
SPICY FISH STEW

Calories	Servings	Prep Time	Cook Time
300	4	15M	30M

INGREDIENTS:

- 1 whole fish (such as red snapper or mackerel), cleaned and cut into large pieces
- 8 cups water
- 4 slices of ginger
- 2 cloves garlic, minced
- 1 onion, sliced
- 1 small daikon radish, peeled and sliced
- 1/2 large carrot, sliced
- 1/2 zucchini, sliced
- 4-6 shiitake mushrooms, sliced
- 2-3 stalks of green onions, cut into 2-inch pieces
- 2 tablespoons gochugaru (Korean red pepper flakes, adjust to taste)
- 2 tablespoons gochujang (Korean red pepper paste)
- 2 tablespoons soy sauce
- 1 tablespoon fish sauce
- 1 tablespoon sesame oil
- Salt and black pepper to taste
- 1 block of tofu, cut into cubes
- Sliced red and green chili peppers (for garnish, optional)
- Sliced garlic chives (buchu) for garnish (optional)

DIRECTIONS:

1. In a large pot, add the cleaned and cut fish, water, ginger slices, and minced garlic. Bring it to a boil, then reduce the heat and let it simmer for about 10-15 minutes to create a fish broth. Skim off any impurities that rise to the surface.

2. Remove the fish pieces from the broth and set them aside.

3. Add the sliced onion, daikon radish, carrot, zucchini, shiitake mushrooms, and green onions to the pot. Continue to simmer until the vegetables are tender, which should take about 10-15 minutes.

4. In a small bowl, combine gochugaru (Korean red pepper flakes), gochujang (Korean red pepper paste), soy sauce, fish sauce, and sesame oil to make the seasoning paste.

5. Add the seasoning paste to the pot and stir well to combine. Adjust the spiciness to your liking by adding more gochugaru if needed.

6. Return the cooked fish to the pot and gently simmer for an additional 5-10 minutes to infuse the flavors.

7. Add the tofu cubes and cook for a few more minutes until heated through.

8. Season with salt and black pepper to taste.

9. Serve your Spicy Fish Stew (Maeuntang) hot, garnished with sliced red and green chili peppers and garlic chives if desired.

Calories	Servings	Prep Time	Cook Time
250	4	30M	30M

INGREDIENTS:

- 4 small to medium-sized squid
- 1 cup glutinous rice (chapssal)
- 1/2 cup ground pork
- 1/2 cup kimchi, finely chopped
- 1/4 cup leek, finely chopped
- 1/4 cup onion, finely chopped
- 2 cloves garlic, minced
- 2 tablespoons soy sauce
- 1 tablespoon gochugaru (Korean red pepper flakes)
- 1 tablespoon sesame oil
- 1/2 teaspoon salt
- 1/4 teaspoon black pepper
- 1 tablespoon vegetable oil (for frying)
- Toothpicks (for sealing)

DIRECTIONS:

1. Start by preparing the squid. Clean and gut the squid, removing the cartilage inside. Rinse them thoroughly, inside and out. Pat them dry with a paper towel.

2. In a bowl, combine glutinous rice (chapssal) with enough water to soak it for about 30 minutes. Drain and set aside.

3. In a separate bowl, mix the ground pork, chopped kimchi, leek, onion, minced garlic, soy sauce, gochugaru (Korean red pepper flakes), sesame oil, salt, and black pepper.

4. Stuff each squid with the soaked glutinous rice and the pork mixture. Seal the openings with toothpicks.

5. Heat vegetable oil in a large pan over medium-high heat. Carefully add the stuffed squids and cook them until they are golden brown, turning them occasionally. This should take about 20-30 minutes, or until the squid is cooked through and the stuffing is no longer pink.

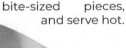

6. Once the Ojingeo Sundae is cooked, remove the toothpicks, slice the stuffed squids into bite-sized pieces, and serve hot.

Calories	Servings	Prep Time	Cook Time
300	4	20M	1H30M

INGREDIENTS:

- 1.5 lbs (700 g) beef short ribs
- 8 cups water
- 1 onion, sliced
- 4 cloves garlic, minced
- 1 small daikon radish, peeled and sliced
- 2 carrots, sliced
- 1 leek, sliced
- 1 tablespoon soy sauce
- Salt and pepper to taste
- Sliced green onions (for garnish)
- Cooked white rice (for serving)

DIRECTIONS:

1. Start by blanching the beef short ribs. Place them in a large pot and cover with water. Bring the water to a boil and cook for about 5 minutes. Drain and rinse the ribs to remove any impurities.

2. In the same large pot, add the blanched beef short ribs, 8 cups of water, sliced onion, minced garlic, and soy sauce. Bring it to a boil, then reduce the heat to low and simmer for about 1 hour until the meat becomes tender.

3. Skim off any foam or impurities that rise to the surface during cooking.

4. Add the sliced daikon radish and carrots to the pot. Continue to simmer for an additional 20-30 minutes until the vegetables are tender.

5. Season the soup with salt and pepper to taste.

6. Just before serving, add the sliced leek to the soup and cook for a few more minutes until it wilts.

7. Serve your Short Rib Soup (Kalbi Tang) hot, garnished with sliced green onions. It's traditionally enjoyed with a side of cooked white rice.

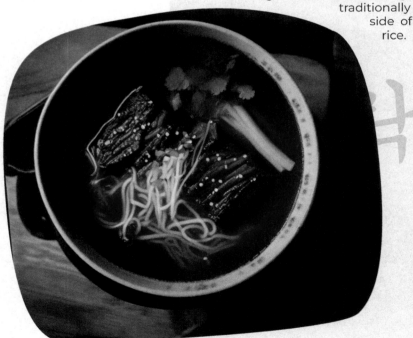

Calories	Servings	Prep Time	Cook Time
60	4	10M	15M

INGREDIENTS:

- 1 lb (500 g) of fresh deodeok roots
- 2 tablespoons soy sauce
- 1 tablespoon sugar
- 1 tablespoon mirin (rice wine)
- 1 teaspoon minced garlic
- 1 teaspoon sesame oil
- 1/2 teaspoon gochugaru (Korean red pepper flakes, adjust to taste)
- 1/4 teaspoon black pepper
- Vegetable oil for grilling

DIRECTIONS:

1. Start by cleaning and peeling the deodeok roots. Rinse them under cold water to remove any dirt or impurities. Pat them dry with a paper towel.

2. In a bowl, combine soy sauce, sugar, mirin, minced garlic, sesame oil, gochugaru (Korean red pepper flakes), and black pepper. Mix well to create a marinade.

3. Place the cleaned deodeok roots in a shallow dish and pour the marinade over them. Make sure the roots are coated evenly. Let them marinate for about 10 minutes.

4. Heat a grill or grill pan over medium-high heat. Brush the grill grates with vegetable oil to prevent sticking.

5. Grill the marinated deodeok roots for about 5-7 minutes, turning occasionally until they become tender and develop a slightly charred appearance.

6. Serve your Grilled Deodeok Root hot as a delicious and healthy Korean side dish.

Calories	Servings	Prep Time	Cook Time
120	4	10M	15M

INGREDIENTS:

- 4 large eggs
- 1/2 cup water
- 1/4 teaspoon salt
- 1/4 teaspoon sugar
- 1/4 teaspoon sesame oil
- 1/4 cup chopped scallions (optional)
- 1/4 cup chopped bell peppers (optional)
- 1/4 cup chopped onions (optional)
- 1/4 cup chopped mushrooms (optional)
- 1/4 cup shredded cheese (optional)
- Cooking spray or vegetable oil (for greasing)

DIRECTIONS:

1. In a mixing bowl, crack the eggs and whisk them until the yolks and whites are well combined.

2. Add water, salt, sugar, and sesame oil to the eggs and continue to whisk until everything is evenly mixed.

3. Grease a heatproof dish or ramekin with cooking spray or a small amount of vegetable oil.

4. If you're using any optional ingredients like scallions, bell peppers, onions, mushrooms, or cheese, scatter them evenly on the bottom of the dish.

5. Pour the egg mixture over the optional ingredients, filling the dish to about 3/4 full.

6. Create a steaming setup by placing a steamer rack or a trivet in a large pot. Fill the pot with about 1 inch of water and bring it to a simmer.

7. Carefully place the dish with the egg mixture on the rack or trivet in the pot. Cover the pot and steam the egg for about 10-15 minutes or until it's set. You can check doneness by inserting a toothpick; it should come out clean when the egg is fully cooked.

8. Remove the dish from the pot and let it cool for a few minutes.

9. Serve your Steamed Egg hot as a classic Korean side dish or appetizer.

Calories	Servings	Prep Time	Cook Time
220	4	20M	0M

INGREDIENTS:

- 1/2 lb (250 g) fresh beef sirloin or tenderloin, finely minced
- 1 egg yolk
- 2 cloves garlic, minced
- 1/2 small Asian pear, grated
- 2 tablespoons soy sauce
- 1 tablespoon honey
- 1/2 tablespoon sesame oil
- 1/2 tablespoon toasted sesame seeds
- 1/2 tablespoon finely chopped green onion
- 1/2 teaspoon finely minced ginger
- 1/4 teaspoon black pepper
- Sliced cucumber, pear, or lettuce (for garnish)
- Toasted pine nuts (for garnish, optional)
- Korean red pepper powder (gochugaru, for garnish, optional)

DIRECTIONS:

1. In a mixing bowl, combine the finely minced beef, egg yolk, and minced garlic. Mix well.

2. Add the grated Asian pear to the mixture, which will help tenderize the beef. Stir until everything is well combined.

3. In a separate bowl, prepare the sauce by mixing soy sauce, honey, sesame oil, toasted sesame seeds, green onion, minced ginger, and black pepper.

4. Combine the sauce with the beef mixture and mix thoroughly to ensure the beef is coated with the sauce.

5. Place the Yukhoe on a serving plate and garnish it with sliced cucumber, pear, or lettuce, and toasted pine nuts if desired.

6. Optionally, you can sprinkle a bit of Korean red pepper powder (gochugaru) over the dish for a hint of spice.

7. Serve your Korean Beef Tartare cold as an appetizer or a side dish, traditionally enjoyed with a bowl of rice.

Calories	Servings	Prep Time	Cook Time
350	4	30M	1H0M

Ingredients:

- 1 lb (500 g) beef or pork tripe, cleaned and sliced
- 1 lb (500 g) beef or pork belly, sliced
- 4 cups beef or pork broth
- 1 onion, sliced
- 1 leek, sliced
- 4-6 shiitake mushrooms, sliced
- 1 small daikon radish, peeled and sliced
- 1 small carrot, sliced
- 2-3 slices of Korean rice cakes (tteok)
- 1/2 cup sliced kimchi
- 2 tablespoons gochugaru (Korean red pepper flakes)
- 2 tablespoons gochujang (Korean red pepper paste)
- 2 tablespoons soy sauce
- 1 tablespoon minced garlic
- 1 tablespoon sesame oil
- 1/2 tablespoon sugar
- Salt and black pepper to taste
- Sliced scallions and enoki mushrooms (for garnish, optional)

Directions:

1. In a large hot pot or a Korean earthenware pot, add the beef or pork belly slices and cook them until they release some fat and become slightly browned.

2. Add the sliced beef or pork tripe to the pot and stir-fry them for a few minutes until they start to change color.

3. Pour the beef or pork broth into the pot and bring it to a boil.

4. Add the sliced onion, leek, shiitake mushrooms, daikon radish, carrot, Korean rice cakes (tteok), and kimchi to the pot. Stir to combine.

5. In a separate bowl, prepare a sauce by mixing gochugaru (Korean red pepper flakes), gochujang (Korean red pepper paste), soy sauce, minced garlic, sesame oil, sugar, and a bit of water to thin it out.

6. Pour the sauce into the pot and stir well to distribute the flavors. Adjust the spiciness with more gochugaru if needed.

7. Let the hot pot simmer for about 20-30 minutes until all the ingredients are cooked and tender.

8. Season with salt and black pepper to taste.

9. Optionally, garnish with sliced scallions and enoki mushrooms for extra flavor.

10. Serve your Tripe Hot Pot (Gopchang Jeongol) hot and enjoy the rich and hearty flavors.

Calories	Servings	Prep Time	Cook Time
250	4	15M	15M

INGREDIENTS:

- 1 lb (500 g) boneless, skinless chicken thighs, thinly sliced
- 1/2 onion, thinly sliced
- 2 green onions, chopped
- 1 small carrot, julienned
- 4 cloves garlic, minced
- 1/4 cup soy sauce
- 2 tablespoons gochugaru (Korean red pepper flakes)
- 2 tablespoons gochujang (Korean red pepper paste)
- 2 tablespoons honey
- 1 tablespoon sesame oil
- 1 tablespoon mirin (rice wine)
- 1/2 tablespoon sugar
- 1/2 teaspoon minced ginger
- Vegetable oil (for cooking)
- Sesame seeds (for garnish, optional)

DIRECTIONS:

1. In a mixing bowl, combine the minced garlic, soy sauce, gochugaru (Korean red pepper flakes), gochujang (Korean red pepper paste), honey, sesame oil, mirin, sugar, and minced ginger. Mix well to create a marinade.

2. Add the thinly sliced chicken to the marinade and ensure it's well coated. Let it marinate for at least 10 minutes to allow the flavors to infuse.

3. Heat a large skillet or grill pan over medium-high heat. Add a bit of vegetable oil to prevent sticking.

4. Add the marinated chicken and stir-fry or grill it for about 5-7 minutes or until it's cooked through.

5. Add the thinly sliced onion, julienned carrot, and chopped green onions to the pan and continue to stir-fry for another 3-4 minutes until the vegetables are tender.

6. Garnish your Spicy Chicken BBQ with sesame seeds if desired.

7. Serve your Dak Bulgogi hot with a side of steamed rice and your favorite Korean banchan (side dishes).

Calories	Servings	Prep Time	Cook Time
350	4	30M	15M

INGREDIENTS:

- 4 whole eels, cleaned and gutted
- 1/4 cup soy sauce
- 1/4 cup mirin (rice wine)
- 2 tablespoons honey
- 2 tablespoons sesame oil
- 2 cloves garlic, minced
- 1 teaspoon grated ginger
- 1/2 teaspoon sesame seeds
- Salt and black pepper to taste
- Sliced green onions (for garnish)
- Lemon wedges (for serving)

DIRECTIONS:

1. Start by preparing the eels. Make sure they are cleaned and gutted. Rinse them thoroughly under cold water and pat them dry with paper towels.

2. In a bowl, combine soy sauce, mirin, honey, sesame oil, minced garlic, grated ginger, sesame seeds, salt, and black pepper. Mix well to create a marinade.

3. Place the eels in a shallow dish and pour the marinade over them. Make sure the eels are evenly coated with the marinade. Let them marinate for about 20-30 minutes.

4. Preheat your grill to medium-high heat. Make sure the grates are clean and well-oiled to prevent sticking.

5. Place the marinated eels on the grill, skin-side down. Grill them for about 6-8 minutes on each side, or until they are cooked through and have a slightly charred appearance.

6. Baste the eels with any remaining marinade while grilling to keep them moist and flavorful.

7. Garnish your Grilled Eel with sliced green onions and serve it with lemon wedges on the side.

8. Enjoy your Jangeo Gui hot as a delectable Korean seafood dish.

Calories	Servings	Prep Time	Cook Time
400	4	30M	1H30M

INGREDIENTS:

- 2 lbs (900 g) beef short ribs, cut into 2-inch pieces
- 1 onion, sliced
- 4 cloves garlic, minced
- 1 carrot, sliced
- 1 daikon radish, peeled and sliced
- 4-6 shiitake mushrooms, sliced
- 1/4 cup soy sauce
- 2 tablespoons sugar
- 2 tablespoons mirin (rice wine)
- 2 tablespoons sesame oil
- 1 tablespoon honey
- 1/2 tablespoon grated ginger
- 1/4 teaspoon black pepper
- 4 cups water
- Sliced green onions (for garnish)
- Toasted sesame seeds (for garnish, optional)

DIRECTIONS:

1. In a large pot, bring 4 cups of water to a boil. Add the beef short ribs and cook for about 3-5 minutes to remove any impurities. Drain and rinse the ribs.

2. In the same pot, place the parboiled beef ribs, sliced onion, minced garlic, carrot, daikon radish, and shiitake mushrooms.

3. In a bowl, mix soy sauce, sugar, mirin, sesame oil, honey, grated ginger, and black pepper to create a sauce.

4. Pour the sauce over the ingredients in the pot.

5. Bring the mixture to a boil, then reduce the heat to low. Cover and simmer for about 1 hour or until the beef is tender.

6. Occasionally skim off any foam that forms on the surface during cooking.

7. Once the beef is tender and the flavors have melded, garnish with sliced green onions and toasted sesame seeds if desired.

8. Serve your Braised Short Ribs (Galbijjim) hot with steamed rice and your choice of Korean banchan (side dishes).

Calories	Servings	Prep Time	Cook Time
180	4	20M	10M

INGREDIENTS:

- 1 lb (500 g) small octopus (nakji), cleaned and prepared
- 1 onion, thinly sliced
- 1 red bell pepper, thinly sliced
- 1 green bell pepper, thinly sliced
- 4 cloves garlic, minced
- 2 tablespoons gochugaru (Korean red pepper flakes)
- 2 tablespoons soy sauce
- 2 tablespoons mirin (rice wine)
- 1 tablespoon sugar
- 1 tablespoon sesame oil
- 1/2 tablespoon minced ginger
- 1/2 tablespoon toasted sesame seeds
- Vegetable oil (for cooking)
- Sliced scallions (for garnish, optional)

DIRECTIONS:

1. Begin by preparing the octopus. If using whole small octopuses, clean them and remove the heads, then chop them into bite-sized pieces. If using pre-prepared octopus, ensure it's thawed and ready for cooking.

2. In a bowl, combine gochugaru (Korean red pepper flakes), soy sauce, mirin (rice wine), sugar, sesame oil, minced ginger, and toasted sesame seeds. Mix well to create a sauce.

3. Heat a large skillet or wok over medium-high heat and add a bit of vegetable oil.

4. Add the minced garlic and stir-fry for about 30 seconds until fragrant.

5. Add the sliced onion and stir-fry for 2-3 minutes until it begins to soften.

6. Add the prepared octopus to the pan and stir-fry for about 5 minutes until it's cooked through.

7. Add the red and green bell pepper slices and continue to stir-fry for an additional 3-4 minutes until the peppers are tender.

8. Pour the sauce over the cooked octopus and vegetables. Stir well to ensure everything is coated with the sauce and heated through.

9. Garnish your Stir-Fried Octopus (Nakji Bokkeum) with sliced scallions if desired.

10. Serve your Nakji Bokkeum hot as a delicious Korean seafood dish, traditionally enjoyed with a bowl of steamed rice.

Calories	Servings	Prep Time	Cook Time
200	4	20M	30M

INGREDIENTS:

- 12-16 oz (500 g) of mixed mushrooms (shiitake, oyster, enoki, button, etc.), cleaned and sliced
- 1 onion, thinly sliced
- 2-3 cloves garlic, minced
- 1 carrot, julienned
- 1 zucchini, sliced
- 4 cups vegetable or mushroom broth
- 2 tablespoons soy sauce
- 2 tablespoons mirin (rice wine)
- 1 tablespoon sesame oil
- 1/2 tablespoon gochugaru (Korean red pepper flakes, adjust to taste)
- 1/2 tablespoon sugar
- Salt and black pepper to taste
- Tofu, sliced (optional)
- Sliced scallions (for garnish, optional)
- Sliced red chili (for garnish, optional)

DIRECTIONS:

1. In a large hot pot or Korean earthenware pot, add the sliced mushrooms, onion, minced garlic, carrot, and zucchini.

2. In a separate bowl, combine vegetable or mushroom broth, soy sauce, mirin, sesame oil, gochugaru (Korean red pepper flakes), sugar, salt, and black pepper to create a flavorful broth.

3. Pour the broth over the mushrooms and vegetables in the pot.

4. Place the pot on the stove and bring it to a boil. Reduce the heat to a simmer and let it cook for about 20-30 minutes until the vegetables are tender.

5. If desired, add sliced tofu to the hot pot and let it cook for an additional 5 minutes.

6. Garnish your Mushroom Hot Pot (Beoseot Jeongol) with sliced scallions and red chili if you like a bit of extra heat.

7. Serve your Beoseot Jeongol hot as a delightful Korean hot pot dish, perfect for sharing with friends and family.

Calories	Servings	Prep Time	Cook Time
250	4	15M	15M

INGREDIENTS:

- 8 oz (250 g) dried somen noodles or wheat noodles
- 2 cups unsweetened soy milk
- 2 cups cold water
- 1/2 cup roasted unsalted peanuts
- 1/4 cup pine nuts
- 3-4 cloves garlic
- 1 teaspoon salt
- 1 teaspoon sugar
- 1 cucumber, julienned
- 1 small zucchini, julienned
- 1/2 cup fresh bean sprouts
- 1 tablespoon toasted sesame seeds (for garnish, optional)
- Fresh mint leaves (for garnish, optional)

DIRECTIONS:

1. Start by boiling the noodles according to the package instructions. Once cooked, rinse them under cold running water and set aside.

2. In a blender, combine the unsweetened soy milk, cold water, roasted peanuts, pine nuts, garlic, salt, and sugar. Blend until you have a smooth and creamy mixture.

3. Strain the soy milk mixture through a fine mesh strainer or cheesecloth to remove any solid particles. You should be left with a smooth soy milk.

4. In a large bowl, combine the cooked and rinsed noodles with the fresh bean sprouts, julienned cucumber, and zucchini.

5. Pour the soy milk over the noodle and vegetable mixture.

6. Give it a good stir to ensure everything is well combined.

7. Garnish your Soy Milk Noodle Soup (Kongguksu) with toasted sesame seeds and fresh mint leaves if desired.

8. Serve your Kongguksu cold and enjoy the refreshing and creamy flavors of this Korean noodle soup.

Calories	Servings	Prep Time	Cook Time
250	4	15M	30M

INGREDIENTS:

- 8 cups water
- 4 oz (100 g) napa cabbage kimchi, chopped
- 4 oz (100 g) beef brisket or pork belly, thinly sliced
- 1/2 cup mung bean sprouts
- 4 garlic cloves, minced
- 1 tablespoon soy sauce
- 1 tablespoon Korean red pepper flakes (gochugaru)
- 1 tablespoon sesame oil
- 1/2 teaspoon salt
- 1/2 teaspoon sugar
- 4 large eggs
- Cooked rice (for serving)
- Sliced green onions (for garnish)
- Sliced Korean radish (mu) or daikon radish (for garnish, optional)

DIRECTIONS:

1. In a large pot, bring 8 cups of water to a boil.

2. Add the chopped napa cabbage kimchi to the boiling water and cook for about 10 minutes.

3. Add the sliced beef brisket or pork belly to the pot and let it cook for an additional 10 minutes until the meat is fully cooked.

4. While the meat is cooking, blanch the mung bean sprouts in boiling water for about 1-2 minutes. Drain and set aside.

5. In a small bowl, mix minced garlic, soy sauce, Korean red pepper flakes (gochugaru), sesame oil, salt, and sugar to create a spicy seasoning.

6. Add the seasoned sauce to the pot and stir well.

7. Crack the eggs into the pot and gently stir to create egg ribbons.

8. Serve your Haejangguk hot with a side of cooked rice and garnish with sliced green onions and Korean radish (mu) or daikon radish if desired.

9. Enjoy your Haejangguk as a comforting hangover cure or a hearty Korean soup!

Calories	Servings	Prep Time	Cook Time
400	4	30M	20M

INGREDIENTS:

- 12 oz (350 g) of pork (loin or tenderloin), thinly sliced into bite-sized pieces
- 1/2 cup potato starch or cornstarch
- 1 egg, beaten
- Vegetable oil (for frying)
- 1 green bell pepper, cut into chunks
- 1 red bell pepper, cut into chunks
- 1 small onion, cut into chunks
- 1 carrot, thinly sliced
- 1 cup canned pineapple chunks, drained
- 1/4 cup ketchup
- 2 tablespoons vinegar
- 2 tablespoons sugar
- 2 tablespoons soy sauce
- 1/2 cup water
- 1 tablespoon cornstarch (for the sauce)
- 2 cloves garlic, minced
- 1/2 teaspoon ginger, minced

DIRECTIONS:

1. Start by preparing the pork. Season the pork slices with a pinch of salt and pepper.

2. Dredge the seasoned pork slices in potato starch or cornstarch, then dip them into the beaten egg.

3. Heat vegetable oil in a deep pan or wok for frying. When the oil is hot (around 350°F or 175°C), add the pork slices in batches and fry until they are golden brown and crispy. Remove the fried pork and place them on a paper towel to drain excess oil.

4. In a separate pan, heat a small amount of vegetable oil and sauté the minced garlic and ginger until fragrant.

5. Add the green and red bell peppers, onion, and carrot chunks to the pan and stir-fry for a few minutes until they start to soften.

6. In a bowl, combine ketchup, vinegar, sugar, soy sauce, and water to create the sweet and sour sauce.

7. In a separate small bowl, mix 1 tablespoon of cornstarch with a little water to create a slurry.

8. Pour the sweet and sour sauce into the pan with the sautéed vegetables. Bring it to a simmer.

9. Stir in the cornstarch slurry and continue to simmer until the sauce thickens.

10. Add the pineapple chunks and the fried pork to the sauce. Stir well to coat everything with the sweet and sour sauce.

11. Serve your Tangsuyuk hot and enjoy the delightful combination of crispy pork and sweet and tangy sauce.

Calories	Servings	Prep Time	Cook Time
350	4	30M	1H

INGREDIENTS:

- 1 whole young chicken (about 3-4 lbs / 1.5 kg)
- 8-10 cloves garlic
- 8-10 jujubes (Korean red dates)
- 2-3 fresh ginseng roots, washed and soaked (or dried ginseng roots)
- 2 cups glutinous rice
- 8-10 chestnuts (optional)
- Salt and black pepper to taste
- Toasted sesame seeds (for garnish, optional)
- Sliced green onions (for garnish, optional)

DIRECTIONS:

1. Rinse the glutinous rice in cold water, then drain and set it aside.

2. Clean the whole young chicken thoroughly. Remove any excess fat and innards. Stuff the chicken cavity with the cleaned glutinous rice, garlic cloves, jujubes, fresh ginseng roots, and chestnuts if you're using them.

3. Sew the chicken cavity shut using kitchen twine or toothpicks to keep the stuffing inside.

4. Place the stuffed chicken in a large pot and add enough water to fully submerge it. You can add more water if needed to ensure the chicken is covered.

5. Bring the water to a boil, then reduce the heat to a simmer. Cook the Samgyetang for about 45-60 minutes or until the chicken is tender and fully cooked.

6. Season the soup with salt and black pepper to taste.

7. Serve your Samgyetang hot in individual bowls, garnished with toasted sesame seeds and sliced green onions if desired.

8. Enjoy this nourishing and comforting Korean Ginseng Chicken Soup!

Calories	Servings	Prep Time	Cook Time
400	4	45M	20M

INGREDIENTS:

- 2 lbs (900 g) of chicken wings or drumettes
- Vegetable oil (for frying)
- 1 cup all-purpose flour
- 1/2 cup cornstarch
- 1 teaspoon baking powder
- 1 teaspoon salt
- 1/2 teaspoon black pepper
- 1 cup cold water
- 1/2 cup gochujang (Korean red pepper paste)
- 1/4 cup ketchup
- 2 tablespoons soy sauce
- 2 tablespoons rice vinegar
- 2 tablespoons honey
- 3 cloves garlic, minced
- 1 teaspoon grated ginger
- Sesame seeds (for garnish, optional)
- Sliced green onions (for garnish, optional)

DIRECTIONS:

1. In a large mixing bowl, combine the all-purpose flour, cornstarch, baking powder, salt, and black pepper.

2. Gradually add the cold water and whisk until you have a smooth batter. The batter should be thick enough to coat the back of a spoon.

3. Heat vegetable oil in a deep pot or large skillet to 350°F (175°C).

4. Dip each chicken wing or drumette into the batter, allowing any excess to drip off.

5. Carefully place the battered chicken pieces into the hot oil and fry until they are golden brown and cooked through. This should take about 8-10 minutes. Fry the chicken in batches, so you don't overcrowd the pot.

6. While the chicken is frying, prepare the spicy sauce. In a separate bowl, mix together gochujang, ketchup, soy sauce, rice vinegar, honey, minced garlic, and grated ginger.

7. Once the chicken is done frying, transfer it to a paper towel-lined plate to drain any excess oil.

8. In a large mixing bowl, toss the fried chicken in the spicy sauce until it's evenly coated.

9. Serve your Yangnyeom Tongdak hot, garnished with sesame seeds and sliced green onions if desired.

10. Enjoy the perfect combination of crispy, spicy, and savory Korean fried chicken!

Calories	Servings	Prep Time	Cook Time
100	4	2H	30M

INGREDIENTS:

- 1 cup acorn starch (dotori garu)
- 3 cups water
- 1/2 teaspoon salt
- 1/2 cup diced cucumber
- 1/2 cup diced carrots
- 1/2 cup sliced bell peppers (red, green, or yellow)
- 1/2 cup sliced scallions
- 1/4 cup soy sauce
- 2 tablespoons rice vinegar
- 2 tablespoons sugar
- 1 tablespoon sesame oil
- 1 tablespoon sesame seeds (for garnish, optional)

DIRECTIONS:

1. Begin by preparing the acorn starch. Rinse the acorns in cold water, then place them in a pot with enough water to cover. Bring the water to a boil and simmer for about 10 minutes. Drain and repeat this process two more times. This helps remove any bitterness.

2. Once the acorns are rinsed and parboiled, dry them thoroughly. Then, grind them into a fine powder using a blender or food processor. This will be your acorn starch.

3. In a bowl, combine the acorn starch with 3 cups of water. Stir well to create a milky mixture.

4. Strain the mixture through a fine-mesh strainer into a clean pot. This helps remove any remaining impurities.

5. Place the pot on the stovetop and cook the mixture over medium heat, stirring constantly. It will begin to thicken. When it reaches a pudding-like consistency, remove it from the heat.

6. Pour the thickened mixture into a container or mold. Allow it to cool, then refrigerate for about 2 hours or until it has set into a jelly-like texture.

7. While the acorn jelly is setting, prepare the sauce. In a bowl, mix soy sauce, rice vinegar, sugar, and sesame oil. Adjust the flavors to your liking.

8. Once the acorn jelly has set, remove it from the container and cut it into bite-sized pieces.

9. Arrange the acorn jelly pieces on a serving plate and garnish with diced cucumber, carrots, bell peppers, and scallions.

10. Drizzle the sauce over the dotorimuk and garnish with sesame seeds if desired.

11. Serve your Dotorimuk cold and enjoy this unique and healthy Korean dish.

Calories	Servings	Prep Time	Cook Time
150	4	10M	10M

INGREDIENTS:

- 4 large eggs
- 2 tablespoons milk
- 1/4 teaspoon salt
- 1/4 teaspoon black pepper
- 1/4 cup finely chopped scallions
- 1/4 cup finely chopped bell peppers (red, green, or yellow)
- 1/4 cup finely chopped onions
- 1/4 cup finely chopped carrots
- 1/4 cup finely chopped ham or cooked bacon (optional)
- 2 tablespoons vegetable oil

DIRECTIONS:

1. Crack the eggs into a bowl and beat them thoroughly.

2. Add milk, salt, and black pepper to the beaten eggs. Mix well.

3. Heat a non-stick skillet or omelette pan over medium-low heat. Add 1 tablespoon of vegetable oil and let it heat up.

4. Pour half of the egg mixture into the skillet, swirling it around to ensure an even layer.

5. As the edges of the omelette begin to set, add half of the chopped scallions, bell peppers, onions, carrots, and ham or cooked bacon (if using). Distribute them evenly over the omelette.

6. Gently lift one edge of the omelette with a spatula and start rolling it tightly. Roll it away from you, and when you reach the other edge, push it back to the starting point, creating a rolled shape.

7. Push the rolled omelette to one side of the skillet and add the remaining 1 tablespoon of vegetable oil to the empty side.

8. Pour the remaining egg mixture into the empty side of the skillet, allowing it to spread and cover the bottom evenly.

9. As the edges of the new omelette begin to set, add the remaining chopped vegetables and ham or cooked bacon.

10. Roll the second omelette tightly in the same manner as the first one.

11. Transfer the rolled omelettes to a cutting board and let them cool for a few minutes.

12. Slice the Gyeran Mari into bite-sized pieces, and arrange them on a serving plate.

13. Serve your Gyeran Mari warm or at room temperature.

Calories	Servings	Prep Time	Cook Time
200	4	10M	15M

INGREDIENTS:

- 4 whole mackerel, cleaned and gutted
- 1/4 cup doenjang (Korean fermented soybean paste)
- 2 tablespoons gochugaru (Korean red pepper flakes)
- 2 tablespoons mirin (rice wine)
- 2 tablespoons soy sauce
- 2 tablespoons minced garlic
- 1 tablespoon sugar
- 1 tablespoon sesame oil
- 1 tablespoon sesame seeds (for garnish, optional)
- Sliced green onions (for garnish, optional)

DIRECTIONS:

1. In a bowl, combine doenjang, gochugaru, mirin, soy sauce, minced garlic, sugar, and sesame oil. Mix well to create a marinade.

2. Make 2-3 shallow diagonal cuts on each side of the mackerel. This helps the marinade penetrate and flavors the fish.

3. Coat the mackerel evenly with the marinade, making sure to get it into the cuts and cavities.

4. Let the mackerel marinate for about 10-15 minutes to absorb the flavors.

5. Preheat your grill to medium-high heat. If you don't have a grill, you can also use a grill pan or broil the mackerel in your oven.

6. Grease the grill grates to prevent the mackerel from sticking. Place the marinated mackerel on the grill and cook for about 5-7 minutes on each side, or until the fish is cooked through and has a nice char.

7. While grilling, you can baste the mackerel with any remaining marinade for extra flavor.

8. Once the mackerel is cooked, transfer it to a serving platter.

9. Garnish with sesame seeds and sliced green onions if desired.

10. Serve your Deonjang Gui hot and enjoy the delicious grilled mackerel with bold Korean flavors.

Calories	Servings	Prep Time	Cook Time
400	4	30M	2H

INGREDIENTS:

- 2 lbs (900 g) beef short ribs, cut into 2-inch pieces
- 1 onion, thinly sliced
- 2 carrots, peeled and cut into chunks
- 2 potatoes, peeled and cut into chunks
- 4 cloves garlic, minced
- 1/4 cup soy sauce
- 2 tablespoons sugar
- 1 tablespoon mirin (rice wine)
- 1 tablespoon sesame oil
- 1 teaspoon grated ginger
- 1/2 teaspoon black pepper
- 2 cups water
- 2 green onions, chopped (for garnish)
- Toasted sesame seeds (for garnish, optional)

DIRECTIONS:

1. In a large pot, add the beef short ribs and enough water to cover them. Bring to a boil and cook for about 5 minutes to remove excess blood and impurities. Drain and rinse the ribs under cold water.

2. In the same pot, add the blanched short ribs, sliced onion, and minced garlic.

3. In a mixing bowl, combine soy sauce, sugar, mirin, sesame oil, grated ginger, and black pepper. Mix well to create a marinade.

4. Pour the marinade over the short ribs and add 2 cups of water to the pot. Bring to a boil.

5. Reduce the heat to low, cover the pot, and simmer for about 1.5 to 2 hours, or until the short ribs are tender and the sauce has thickened.

6. About 30 minutes before the Galbi Jim is done, add the carrots and potatoes to the pot. Simmer until the vegetables are cooked and the meat is fork-tender.

7. Once the Galbi Jim is ready, transfer it to a serving dish, garnish with chopped green onions and toasted sesame seeds if desired.

8. Serve the Galbi Jim hot with a bowl of steamed rice and your favorite side dishes.

Calories	Servings	Prep Time	Cook Time
300	4	30M	20M

INGREDIENTS:

- 2 cups all-purpose flour
- 1/2 cup water
- 1/2 teaspoon salt
- 4 cups chicken or vegetable broth
- 2 cups cooked chicken or tofu, shredded
- 1 cup zucchini, thinly sliced
- 1 cup carrots, julienned
- 1 cup spinach, blanched and chopped
- 4 cloves garlic, minced
- 2 tablespoons soy sauce
- 1 tablespoon sesame oil
- 1 tablespoon vegetable oil
- Salt and pepper to taste
- Chopped green onions (for garnish)

DIRECTIONS:

1. In a mixing bowl, combine the all-purpose flour and 1/2 teaspoon of salt. Slowly add 1/2 cup of water while kneading the dough until it comes together. Knead the dough for about 5 minutes until it's smooth and elastic. Cover the dough with a damp cloth and let it rest for 15 minutes.

2. Roll out the dough on a floured surface into a thin sheet, about 1/8-inch thick. You can use a rolling pin or a pasta machine to achieve the desired thickness.

3. Cut the rolled dough into thin strips to make the noodles. You can cut them as wide or as narrow as you like. Toss the noodles with a bit of flour to prevent sticking, and set them aside.

4. In a large pot, heat the vegetable oil over medium heat. Add the minced garlic and sauté for a minute or until fragrant.

5. Pour in the chicken or vegetable broth and bring it to a boil. Once boiling, add the shredded chicken or tofu and let it simmer for a few minutes.

6. Add the sliced zucchini and julienned carrots to the pot. Simmer for an additional 5-7 minutes or until the vegetables are tender.

7. Carefully add the hand-cut noodles to the boiling broth. Cook for about 5-7 minutes or until the noodles are tender and cooked through.

8. Stir in the soy sauce, sesame oil, and season with salt and pepper to taste.

9. Add the blanched and chopped spinach to the soup and simmer for another 2-3 minutes.

10. Serve the Kalguksu hot, garnished with chopped green onions.

Calories	Servings	Prep Time	Cook Time
300	4	1H	3H

INGREDIENTS:

- 2 lbs (900 g) beef ox bones
- 8 cups water
- 1 lbs (450 g) beef brisket
- 1 onion, halved
- 6 cloves garlic
- 2-3 slices of ginger
- Salt to taste
- Cooked white rice
- Chopped green onions (for garnish)
- Kimchi (optional, for serving)

DIRECTIONS:

1. Rinse the beef ox bones under cold running water to remove any impurities. Place the bones in a large pot and add enough water to cover them. Bring to a boil, then reduce the heat and simmer for 10 minutes. Drain the bones and rinse them again.

2. In the same pot, add the parboiled bones, beef brisket, onion, garlic, and ginger.

3. Pour 8 cups of water into the pot and bring it to a boil. Once boiling, reduce the heat to low, cover the pot, and simmer for about 3 hours. Make sure to skim any foam or impurities that rise to the surface.

4. After 3 hours, remove the beef brisket from the pot and let it cool. Once it's cool enough to handle, slice the beef brisket thinly and set it aside.

5. Continue simmering the broth for another hour or until it becomes rich and milky in color. You may need to add more water during this process if the liquid reduces too much.

6. Once the Seolleongtang broth is ready, season it with salt to taste.

7. To serve, place a portion of cooked white rice in each bowl. Add the sliced beef brisket on top of the rice.

8. Ladle the hot Seolleongtang broth into each bowl, covering the rice and beef.

9. Garnish with chopped green onions and serve with kimchi on the side.

Calories	Servings	Prep Time	Cook Time
350	4	1H	10M

INGREDIENTS:

- 8 oz (250g) of dried naengmyeon noodles (buckwheat noodles)
- 4 cups beef or vegetable broth
- 2 cups water
- 3-4 tbsp Korean mustard oil (or to taste)
- 2 tbsp sugar
- 2 tbsp soy sauce
- 1 tbsp rice vinegar
- 1 tsp minced garlic
- 1 cucumber, julienned
- 2 boiled eggs, halved
- 1 Asian pear, julienned
- 1/2 cup pickled radish (optional)
- Ice cubes (optional)

DIRECTIONS:

1. Boil the naengmyeon noodles according to the package instructions. Usually, this involves boiling them for about 3-4 minutes until they're soft but still chewy. Drain and rinse the noodles under cold water to cool them down and remove excess starch. Drain again.

2. In a separate pot, bring the beef or vegetable broth and water to a boil. Let it cool, and then refrigerate it until cold. You want the broth to be very cold.

3. In a small bowl, mix the Korean mustard oil, sugar, soy sauce, rice vinegar, and minced garlic to make the noodle sauce. Adjust the seasoning to your taste. This sauce should be a bit sweet and tangy with a spicy kick from the mustard oil.

4. To serve, divide the cold naengmyeon noodles into individual serving bowls.

5. Pour the cold broth over the noodles. Add ice cubes to the broth if you want it extra cold.

6. Garnish the noodles with julienned cucumber, Asian pear, and boiled egg halves.

7. Add a few slices of pickled radish if desired.

8. Drizzle the mustard sauce over each serving.

9. Mix everything together before eating to enjoy the refreshing flavors of Mul Naengmyeon.

Calories	Servings	Prep Time	Cook Time
350	2	15M	20M

INGREDIENTS:

- 7 oz (200g) fresh or dried jjamppong noodles (or other noodles of your choice)
- 7 oz (200g) mixed seafood (shrimp, mussels, squid, and/or clams)
- 2 tablespoons vegetable oil
- 1 small onion, finely chopped
- 2 cloves garlic, minced
- 1 teaspoon ginger, minced
- 1 tablespoon gochugaru (Korean red pepper flakes) or to taste
- 4 cups chicken or seafood broth
- 2 tablespoons soy sauce
- 1 tablespoon oyster sauce
- 1 teaspoon sugar
- 1/2 teaspoon salt
- 1/2 teaspoon black pepper
- 1/2 cup Napa cabbage, chopped
- 1/2 cup zucchini, thinly sliced
- 2 green onions, chopped
- 1/2 carrot, julienned
- 1/2 red bell pepper, julienned

DIRECTIONS:

1. Cook the jjamppong noodles according to the package instructions. Drain and set them aside.

2. In a large pot, heat the vegetable oil over medium-high heat.

3. Add the chopped onion, minced garlic, and ginger to the pot. Sauté for a few minutes until the onion becomes translucent.

4. Add gochugaru (Korean red pepper flakes) and continue to stir for about a minute to release its flavor and spice.

5. Pour the chicken or seafood broth into the pot and bring it to a boil.

6. Season the broth with soy sauce, oyster sauce, sugar, salt, and black pepper. Adjust the seasonings to your taste.

7. Add the mixed seafood to the boiling broth. Cook for a few minutes until the seafood is almost fully cooked.

8. Add the Napa cabbage, zucchini, green onions, carrot, and red bell pepper to the pot. Cook for an additional 2-3 minutes, allowing the vegetables to become tender.

9. To serve, divide the cooked jjamppong noodles into serving bowls.

10. Ladle the spicy seafood soup and vegetables over the noodles.

11. Garnish with extra green onions or additional gochugaru for added spice if desired.

12. Serve hot and enjoy your homemade jjamppong!

Calories	Servings	Prep Time	Cook Time
150	6	8H	20M

INGREDIENTS:

- 1 cup dried mung beans
- 1/2 small onion, roughly chopped
- 1/2 small carrot, roughly chopped
- 2-3 green onions, chopped
- 1 small red or green chili (optional, for spiciness)
- 1/2 teaspoon salt, or to taste
- 1/4 teaspoon black pepper
- Vegetable oil for frying
- Soy sauce or vinegar dipping sauce (optional)

DIRECTIONS:

1. Rinse the mung beans thoroughly, then place them in a large bowl and cover with water. Allow the beans to soak for at least 8 hours or overnight. This will help soften the beans for blending.

2. Drain the soaked mung beans and place them in a blender or food processor.

3. Add the roughly chopped onion, carrot, and chili (if using) to the blender with the mung beans.

4. Blend the mixture until you have a smooth batter. You may need to scrape down the sides of the blender a few times to ensure even blending.

5. Transfer the batter to a mixing bowl and add the chopped green onions, salt, and black pepper. Mix well to combine.

6. In a non-stick skillet or frying pan, heat a small amount of vegetable oil over medium-high heat.

7. Pour a ladleful of the mung bean batter into the hot skillet, spreading it out into a thin, round pancake.

8. Cook for about 2-3 minutes on each side, or until the pancake is golden brown and crispy.

9. Repeat the process with the remaining batter, adding more oil to the skillet as needed.

10. Serve the mung bean pancakes hot, with soy sauce or vinegar dipping sauce if desired.

Calories	Servings	Prep Time	Cook Time
200	4	30M	15M

INGREDIENTS:

- 2 whole fish (such as mackerel, trout, or sea bream), cleaned and gutted
- 2 tablespoons vegetable oil
- Salt, to taste
- Black pepper, to taste
- 2-3 cloves of garlic, minced
- 1-2 green chilies (optional, for spiciness)
- 1 lemon, cut into wedges
- Soy sauce or dipping sauce (for serving)

DIRECTIONS:

1. Preheat your grill to medium-high heat. Make sure the grates are clean and well-oiled to prevent the fish from sticking.

2. Rinse the fish under cold water and pat them dry with paper towels.

3. Make shallow diagonal cuts on both sides of the fish, about 1 inch apart. This will help the fish cook evenly and absorb the flavors.

4. Rub the fish with vegetable oil to prevent sticking to the grill grates. Season both sides with salt and black pepper.

5. If you prefer a spicy kick, you can stuff the fish cavity with minced garlic and green chilies.

6. Place the fish on the preheated grill and cook for about 6-7 minutes per side, depending on the thickness of the fish. Grill until the skin is crispy and the flesh is opaque and easily flakes with a fork.

7. While grilling, avoid moving the fish too much to get those beautiful grill marks.

8. Once the fish is cooked through, remove it from the grill and transfer it to a serving platter.

9. Serve the grilled fish hot with lemon wedges and a side of soy sauce or your preferred dipping sauce.

Calories	Servings	Prep Time	Cook Time
250	4	30M	15M

INGREDIENTS:

- 4 large yubu (fried tofu pouches), available in Korean or Asian grocery stores
- 2 cups cooked short-grain white rice
- 1/2 cup pickled radish (danmuji), julienned
- 1/2 cup carrots, julienned
- 1/2 cup cucumber, julienned
- 1/2 cup spinach, blanched and squeezed dry
- 1/2 cup cooked and seasoned ground beef or protein of your choice
- 2 tablespoons sesame oil
- 1 tablespoon soy sauce
- 1 tablespoon rice vinegar
- 1 tablespoon sugar
- 1 teaspoon salt
- 1 teaspoon sesame seeds
- Roasted seaweed (gim) for garnish

DIRECTIONS:

1. Prepare the Yubu:Gently rinse the yubu pouches under cold water to remove excess oil and salt. Squeeze out any excess liquid. Slice them in half to create pockets for stuffing.

2. Prepare the Filling:In a bowl, combine the cooked rice, pickled radish, carrots, cucumber, blanched spinach, and seasoned ground beef. Toss them together.

3. Make the Seasoning Sauce:In a small bowl, mix the sesame oil, soy sauce, rice vinegar, sugar, salt, and sesame seeds to make the seasoning sauce.

4. Stuff the Yubu Pockets:Open each yubu pouch and gently stuff them with the rice and vegetable mixture. Be careful not to overstuff to ensure they can be easily sealed.

5. Drizzle with Seasoning Sauce:Drizzle the prepared seasoning sauce over the stuffed yubu pockets, ensuring the flavors are distributed evenly.

6. Serve and Garnish:Serve the Yubuchobap on a platter and garnish with roasted seaweed (gim) strips for added flavor and presentation.

Calories	Servings	Prep Time	Cook Time
300	4	30M	30M

INGREDIENTS:

- 1 cup sliced tteok (Korean rice cakes)
- 12 dumplings (store-bought or homemade)
- 8 cups beef or vegetable broth
- 1/2 cup sliced Korean radish (mu)
- 2 green onions, chopped
- 2 cloves garlic, minced
- 1/2 teaspoon soy sauce
- Salt and pepper to taste
- Seaweed (gim) for garnish (optional)
- Red pepper flakes (gochugaru) for garnish (optional)

DIRECTIONS:

1. In a large pot, bring the beef or vegetable broth to a boil.

2. Add the sliced tteok (rice cakes) to the boiling broth and cook for about 5-7 minutes or until they become soft and chewy. If using frozen tteok, cook them a bit longer until they float to the surface.

3. While the tteok is cooking, prepare the dumplings according to the package instructions if using store-bought dumplings. If you're making homemade dumplings, you can cook them by boiling or pan-frying.

4. Add the soy sauce, minced garlic, and sliced radish to the pot. Allow the soup to simmer for an additional 5-7 minutes until the radish becomes tender.

5. Season the soup with salt and pepper to taste.

6. Once the tteok, dumplings, and radish are fully cooked, add the cooked dumplings to the soup.

7. Simmer the soup for a few more minutes until the dumplings are heated through.

8. Before serving, garnish the Tteok Mandu Guk with chopped green onions, seaweed (gim) strips, and red pepper flakes (gochugaru) for extra flavor and presentation.

Calories	Servings	Prep Time	Cook Time
250	4	15M	1H30M

INGREDIENTS:

- 1 whole chicken (about 3-4 lbs / 1.5 lg)
- 10 cups water
- 1 onion, halved
- 1 head of garlic, halved
- 1 piece of ginger (about 2 inches), sliced
- 8-10 cups cooked rice
- Salt to taste
- Sliced green onions for garnish
- Toasted sesame seeds for garnish (optional)
- Kimchi and other banchan (side dishes) for serving (optional)

DIRECTIONS:

1. Rinse the whole chicken under cold water and remove any excess fat. Place the chicken in a large stockpot.

2. Add 10 cups of water to the pot, ensuring that the chicken is fully submerged.

3. Add the halved onion, halved garlic head, and sliced ginger to the pot.

4. Bring the water to a boil over high heat, then reduce the heat to low, cover the pot, and let it simmer for about 1 to 1.5 hours, or until the chicken is fully cooked and tender.

5. Skim off any impurities and foam that rise to the surface during simmering.

6. Carefully remove the chicken from the pot and place it on a cutting board. Allow it to cool for a few minutes.

7. While the chicken is cooling, strain the broth to remove the onion, garlic, and ginger. You should be left with a clear and flavorful chicken broth.

8. Once the chicken has cooled enough to handle, shred the meat into bite-sized pieces, discarding the bones and skin.

9. Return the shredded chicken to the pot with the clear broth.

10. Bring the soup back to a simmer and season with salt to taste.

11. To serve, place a scoop of cooked rice into each serving bowl.

12. Ladle the chicken soup over the rice.

13. Garnish with sliced green onions and toasted sesame seeds if desired.

14. Serve Dak Gomtang hot with kimchi and other banchan (side dishes) on the side for a complete meal.

Calories	Servings	Prep Time	Cook Time
250	4	30M	20M

INGREDIENTS:

- 1 lb (450g) small octopus, cleaned and prepared
- 3 tbsp gochugaru (Korean red pepper flakes)
- 2 tbsp soy sauce
- 2 tbsp sugar
- 2 tbsp minced garlic
- 1 tbsp gochujang (Korean red pepper paste)
- 1 tbsp mirin (rice wine)
- 1 tbsp sesame oil
- 1 tbsp vegetable oil
- 1 onion, thinly sliced
- 1 carrot, julienned
- 1 scallion, chopped
- 1 small zucchini, julienned
- Sesame seeds, for garnish
- Cooked rice, for serving

DIRECTIONS:

1. In a bowl, mix together gochugaru (Korean red pepper flakes), soy sauce, sugar, minced garlic, gochujang (Korean red pepper paste), mirin (rice wine), and sesame oil to make the spicy sauce. Adjust the spiciness and sweetness to your preference.

2. In a large skillet or wok, heat the vegetable oil over medium-high heat.

3. Add the sliced onion and stir-fry for about 2 minutes until it becomes translucent.

4. Add the prepared small octopus to the skillet and stir-fry for another 2-3 minutes until they start to curl and turn opaque.

5. Add the julienned carrot and zucchini to the skillet and stir-fry for an additional 2-3 minutes until they begin to soften.

6. Pour the spicy sauce over the octopus and vegetables. Stir-fry everything together for another 3-4 minutes, ensuring the octopus and vegetables are evenly coated with the sauce.

7. Taste and adjust the seasoning, adding more sugar or gochugaru if needed.

8. Add the chopped scallion to the skillet and stir-fry for an additional minute.

9. Remove from heat and transfer the Nakji Bokkeum to a serving plate.

10. Garnish with sesame seeds and serve hot over a bed of steamed rice.

Calories	Servings	Prep Time	Cook Time
250	4	20M	0M

INGREDIENTS:

- 1 lb (450g) fresh sashimi-grade fish (common choices include flounder, halibut, or tuna)
- 1 cucumber, julienned
- 1 daikon radish, julienned
- 1 small carrot, julienned
- 1/4 red onion, thinly sliced
- 1/4 green chili pepper, thinly sliced (optional, for heat)
- 2 tbsp soy sauce
- 1 tbsp sesame oil
- 1 tbsp gochugaru (Korean red pepper flakes)
- 1/2 tsp sugar
- 1/2 tsp minced garlic
- 1/2 tsp minced ginger
- Sesame seeds, for garnish
- Sliced lemon, for garnish
- Fresh perilla leaves (kkaennip), for serving

DIRECTIONS:

1. Begin by preparing the fish. Ensure it's sashimi-grade and fresh. Slice the fish into thin strips or bite-sized pieces. Arrange the fish on a serving platter.

2. Prepare the vegetables. Julienne the cucumber, daikon radish, carrot, and thinly slice the red onion. If you prefer some heat, thinly slice the green chili pepper. Arrange these alongside the fish on the serving platter.

3. In a small bowl, mix together soy sauce, sesame oil, gochugaru (Korean red pepper flakes), sugar, minced garlic, and minced ginger to create the dipping sauce.

4. Serve the Hwae with fresh perilla leaves for wrapping. Each diner can take a perilla leaf, place a piece of fish, some vegetables, and a small amount of dipping sauce. Fold or wrap the perilla leaf and enjoy.

5. Garnish with sesame seeds and a slice of lemon.

Calories	Servings	Prep Time	Cook Time
400	4	30M	20M

INGREDIENTS:

- 4 cups cooked sushi rice
- 1 lb (450g) assorted sashimi-grade fish (e.g., tuna, salmon, yellowtail), thinly sliced
- 1 cup julienned carrots
- 1 cup julienned cucumbers
- 1 cup julienned daikon radish
- 1/2 cup pickled ginger (gari)
- 4 sheets nori (seaweed), toasted and crushed into small pieces
- 4 poached or soft-boiled eggs
- 2 tbsp sesame seeds
- 2 tbsp soy sauce
- 2 tbsp rice vinegar
- 1 tbsp sugar
- 1 tsp sesame oil
- Pickled wasabi (optional)
- Soy sauce and wasabi for serving

DIRECTIONS:

1. In a small bowl, mix together the soy sauce, rice vinegar, sugar, and sesame oil to create a sauce. Set aside.

2. Divide the cooked sushi rice among four serving bowls.

3. Arrange the sliced sashimi-grade fish, julienned carrots, cucumbers, and daikon radish on top of the rice.

4. Place a poached or soft-boiled egg in the center of each bowl.

5. Sprinkle the toasted and crushed nori pieces over the ingredients in each bowl.

6. Drizzle the sauce evenly over the rice and ingredients.

7. Garnish with pickled ginger, sesame seeds, and pickled wasabi if desired.

8. Serve the Hwedeopbap with additional soy sauce and wasabi on the side.

Calories	Servings	Prep Time	Cook Time
150	4	15M	0M

INGREDIENTS:

- 1 block (14 oz or 400g) firm tofu
- 2 cups napa cabbage kimchi, chopped
- 2 green onions, chopped
- 1 clove garlic, minced
- 1 tsp grated ginger
- 1 tbsp gochugaru (Korean red pepper flakes)
- 1 tsp sesame oil
- 1 tsp soy sauce (use a gluten-free soy sauce for a gluten-free option)
- 1/2 tsp sugar
- 1 tsp toasted sesame seeds
- 1 tsp roasted sesame seeds (for garnish)
- Optional: sliced green chili peppers (for added heat)

DIRECTIONS:

1. Start by draining the tofu. Place the block of tofu on a clean kitchen towel or paper towels. Gently press the tofu with your hands to remove excess moisture. You can also place a weight on top of the tofu to help with the draining process.

2. While the tofu is draining, chop the kimchi, green onions, and prepare the garlic and ginger.

3. In a mixing bowl, combine the chopped kimchi, green onions, minced garlic, grated ginger, gochugaru (Korean red pepper flakes), sesame oil, soy sauce, and sugar. Mix well to create a flavorful kimchi sauce.

4. Once the tofu is well-drained, cut it into bite-sized cubes.

5. In a large serving bowl, add the tofu cubes and pour the prepared kimchi sauce over them.

6. Gently toss the tofu and kimchi together until the tofu is well coated with the sauce.

7. Garnish with toasted sesame seeds and, if desired, sliced green chili peppers for extra heat.

8. Serve your Tofu Kimchi immediately or let it sit for a while to allow the flavors to meld.

JOKBAL
PIG'S FEET

Calories	Servings	Prep Time	Cook Time
300	4	30M	2H

INGREDIENTS:

- 4 pig's trotters (feet)
- 1 cup of soy sauce
- 1 cup of water
- 1/2 cup of rice wine (mirin)
- 1/2 cup of sugar
- 10 cloves of garlic, minced
- 1 onion, chopped
- 1 piece of ginger, sliced
- 5-6 green onions, chopped
- 2-3 dried red chili peppers (optional, for heat)
- 1 tablespoon of black peppercorns
- 1 tablespoon of sesame oil
- 1 tablespoon of toasted sesame seeds
- Hard-boiled eggs (optional, for garnish)
- Fresh lettuce leaves (for serving)

DIRECTIONS:

1. Begin by thoroughly cleaning the pig's feet. Remove any hair and scrub them clean. Rinse well under cold water.

2. In a large pot, combine the cleaned pig's feet, soy sauce, water, rice wine (mirin), sugar, minced garlic, chopped onion, sliced ginger, dried red chili peppers (if using), and black peppercorns.

3. Bring the mixture to a boil over high heat, and then reduce the heat to a simmer. Cook for about 1.5 to 2 hours, or until the pig's feet are tender and the meat easily pulls away from the bone.

4. Once the pig's feet are tender, remove them from the cooking liquid and allow them to cool slightly.

5. While the pig's feet are cooling, strain and reserve the cooking liquid for later.

6. Once the pig's feet are cool enough to handle, cut them into bite-sized pieces.

7. In a separate saucepan, heat the cooking liquid over medium-high heat. Reduce it to a thicker consistency by simmering for about 10-15 minutes. This will become the jokbal sauce.

8. Place the cut pig's feet on a serving platter, drizzle with the jokbal sauce, and garnish with chopped green onions and toasted sesame seeds.

9. If desired, serve with hard-boiled eggs and fresh lettuce leaves. Jokbal is often enjoyed wrapped in lettuce leaves, similar to ssam.

Calories	Servings	Prep Time	Cook Time
350	4	30M	5M

INGREDIENTS:

- 8 oz (250g) dried buckwheat noodles (memil guksu)
- 1 cup Korean radish (mu), julienned
- 1 cup cucumber, julienned
- 1 cup nashi pear or Asian pear, julienned
- 1/2 cup carrot, julienned
- 1/2 cup red cabbage, thinly sliced (optional, for color)
- 4 hard-boiled eggs, halved
- 1/4 cup toasted sesame seeds
- 4-6 sheets of dried seaweed (nori), crumbled
- Ice cubes
- Korean red chili pepper paste (gochujang), to taste
- For the dressing: 3 tbsp soy sauce
- 3 tbsp water
- 2 tbsp sugar
- 2 tbsp white vinegar
- 1-2 cloves garlic, minced
- 1 tsp toasted sesame oil
- 1/2 tsp grated ginger
- 1/4 tsp black pepper

DIRECTIONS:

1. Cook the dried buckwheat noodles (memil guksu) according to the package instructions. Usually, you'll need to boil them for about 4-5 minutes until they are al dente. Drain and rinse them under cold running water until they are cool. Place the cooked noodles in a large bowl and set them aside.

2. In a separate bowl, combine all the dressing ingredients - soy sauce, water, sugar, white vinegar, minced garlic, toasted sesame oil, grated ginger, and black pepper. Mix well until the sugar is dissolved. Adjust the seasoning to your taste.

3. Pour the dressing over the cooked and rinsed buckwheat noodles. Toss the noodles to ensure they are evenly coated with the dressing.

4. To serve, divide the dressed buckwheat noodles among four serving plates.

5. Arrange the julienned vegetables (Korean radish, cucumber, nashi pear, carrot, and red cabbage) on top of the noodles.

6. Sprinkle toasted sesame seeds and crumbled dried seaweed (nori) over the vegetables.

7. Place half a hard-boiled egg on each plate for garnish.

8. Serve the Makguksu cold with extra dressing and Korean red chili pepper paste (gochujang) on the side for those who prefer it spicier.

9. You can also add ice cubes to the noodles just before serving to keep them cool and refreshing.

Calories	Servings	Prep Time	Cook Time
350	4	30M	30M

INGREDIENTS:

- 12 large raw shrimp, peeled and deveined
- 12 fresh mussels, cleaned and debearded
- 8 fresh clams, scrubbed
- 1/2 lb (225g) firm white fish fillets, such as cod or snapper, cut into chunks
- 8 large sea scallops
- 1/2 lb (225g) squid, cleaned and sliced into rings
- 1/2 lb (225g) octopus, cleaned and cut into bite-sized pieces
- 1 small onion, thinly sliced
- 4-6 cloves garlic, minced
- 1-inch piece of ginger, sliced
- 6 cups seafood or vegetable broth
- 1 cup Korean radish (mu), sliced
- 1 small carrot, sliced
- 2 fresh shiitake mushrooms, sliced
- 1/2 cup Korean or napa cabbage, chopped
- 1/2 bunch of Korean leeks (dae-pa) or green onions, cut into 2-inch pieces
- 2-3 fresh red or green chili peppers, sliced (adjust the quantity to your preferred spice level)
- 4-6 dried Korean red chili peppers (gochu), optional for extra spice
- 1/2 cup Korean glass noodles (dangmyeon), soaked in warm water for 30 minutes and drained
- Salt and pepper to taste
- Soy sauce for dipping
- Korean red chili pepper paste (gochujang) for dipping

DIRECTIONS:

1. Prepare all the seafood ingredients - peel and devein the shrimp, clean the mussels and clams, slice the squid, and cut the octopus into bite-sized pieces.

2. In a large hot pot or Korean earthenware pot (ttukbaegi), arrange the seafood and vegetables in layers. Start with the Korean radish (mu) slices at the bottom. Then, add the carrot, onion, ginger slices, and garlic.

3. Place the seafood on top of the vegetables in an aesthetically pleasing manner. Be creative with the arrangement.

4. Add the Korean leeks (dae-pa) or green onions, fresh and dried chili peppers, and shiitake mushrooms.

5. Pour the seafood or vegetable broth over the ingredients, covering them completely.

6. Cover the pot and place it over medium-high heat. Allow it to come to a boil.

7. Once boiling, add the Korean glass noodles (dangmyeon) to the pot.

8. Reduce the heat to medium, and let the hot pot simmer for about 15-20 minutes until the seafood is cooked and the noodles are tender.

9. Season the hot pot with salt and pepper to taste. You can also add more fresh chili peppers if you prefer a spicier dish.

10. Serve the Haemul Jeongol hot pot at the table. Each guest can enjoy a bowl of the hot pot, along with soy sauce and Korean red chili pepper paste (gochujang) for dipping.

Calories	Servings	Prep Time	Cook Time
50	2	30M	0M

INGREDIENTS:

- 1 small live octopus (approximately 1-2 lbs / 500-900 g)
- Soy sauce
- Sesame oil
- Sesame seeds
- Gochugaru (Korean red pepper flakes)
- Thinly sliced vegetables (such as cucumbers and carrots) for garnish

DIRECTIONS:

1. Begin by preparing your live octopus. It's essential to handle this delicacy with care and respect. In some regions, the octopus may be partially cut into smaller pieces before serving, but for sannakji, it's often served whole.

2. To serve sannakji, the octopus is typically cut into small pieces and served immediately, ensuring the freshness and movement of the tentacles. You can do this with a sharp knife or scissors.

3. Arrange the freshly cut octopus pieces on a plate.

4. In small dipping dishes, prepare a mixture of soy sauce, sesame oil, sesame seeds, and gochugaru (Korean red pepper flakes) for dipping.

5. Serve the sannakji with the dipping sauces and thinly sliced vegetables for garnish.

6. To enjoy sannakji, take a piece, dip it into the sauce, and savor the unique texture and flavor. The tentacles may continue to move even after cutting, so be cautious when eating.

Calories	Servings	Prep Time	Cook Time
200	4	15M	20M

INGREDIENTS:

- 1/3 cup fermented soybean paste (doenjang)
- 8 cups water
- 1 cup tofu, diced into small cubes
- 1/2 cup zucchini, sliced into thin half-moons
- 1/2 cup Korean radish (mu), thinly sliced
- 1/2 cup onion, thinly sliced
- 1/2 cup green chili pepper, sliced (adjust to your preferred level of spiciness)
- 3-4 cloves garlic, minced
- 2 tsp vegetable oil
- 1 tsp sesame oil
- 1 tsp Korean red chili pepper flakes (gochugaru), optional for added spice
- Salt and pepper to taste
- Sliced green onions and Korean red chili peppers for garnish (optional)

DIRECTIONS:

1. In a large pot, heat the vegetable oil over medium heat. Add the minced garlic and sauté for about 1 minute or until fragrant.

2. Add the thinly sliced onion, zucchini, Korean radish, and green chili pepper to the pot. Sauté for an additional 2-3 minutes or until the vegetables start to soften.

3. Pour in 8 cups of water and bring the mixture to a boil.

4. Once boiling, add the fermented soybean paste (doenjang) to the pot. Stir well to dissolve the paste in the broth.

5. Reduce the heat to medium and let the stew simmer for about 10-15 minutes, allowing the flavors to meld together.

6. Add the diced tofu cubes to the stew and let them simmer for another 3-5 minutes, or until they are heated through.

7. If you prefer a slightly spicier stew, you can add the Korean red chili pepper flakes (gochugaru) at this point.

8. Season the stew with salt and pepper to taste. Be mindful of the saltiness of your soybean paste; adjust accordingly.

9. Finish the stew with a drizzle of sesame oil and give it a final stir.

Calories	Servings	Prep Time	Cook Time
120	4	15M	15M

INGREDIENTS:

- 2 fillets of white fish (e.g., cod or pollack), boneless and skinless
- 1 cup all-purpose flour
- 1/2 cup water
- 1/2 cup sliced scallions (green onions)
- 1/4 cup thinly sliced Korean red chili pepper (adjust to your preferred level of spiciness)
- 2 cloves garlic, minced
- 1 tsp grated ginger
- 1/2 tsp salt
- 1/4 tsp black pepper
- Vegetable oil for frying
- Soy sauce or soy sauce with vinegar (dipping sauce)

DIRECTIONS:

1. Cut the white fish fillets into small pieces. Place the fish pieces in a bowl.

2. In a separate bowl, prepare the batter. Combine the all-purpose flour, water, minced garlic, grated ginger, salt, and black pepper. Mix until the batter is smooth and free of lumps.

3. Add the sliced scallions and Korean red chili pepper to the batter and mix well.

4. Pour the batter mixture over the fish pieces and gently combine, ensuring the fish is evenly coated.

5. In a large skillet, heat vegetable oil over medium-high heat. Make sure there's enough oil to cover the bottom of the skillet.

6. Once the oil is hot, drop spoonfuls of the fish and batter mixture into the skillet to form individual pancakes. Use the back of the spoon to gently flatten and shape each pancake.

7. Fry the pancakes for about 3-4 minutes on each side or until they turn golden brown and crispy.

8. Place the cooked pancakes on paper towels to remove excess oil and let them cool slightly.

9. Serve the Saengseon Jeon with a dipping sauce made by mixing soy sauce or soy sauce with vinegar.

Some sample weekly meal plans to help integrate Korean dishes into your routine, based on recipes from this cookbook:

week 1	Sunday	Sundubu Jjigae - Spicy soft tofu stew
	Monday	Bibimbap - Rice bowl with sautéed vegetables, gochujang sauce
	Tuesday	Kimchi Jjigae - Spicy kimchi stew with pork and tofu
	Wednesday	Bulgogi - Marinated grilled beef with lettuce wraps
	Thursday	Japchae - Sweet potato glass noodles stir fry
	Friday	Haemul Pajeon - Seafood and scallion pancake
	Saturday	Sundubu Jjigae - Spicy soft tofu stew
week 2	Sunday	Budae Jjigae - Spicy sausage stew
	Monday	Yukgaejang - Spicy shredded beef soup
	Tuesday	Kimchi Fried Rice - Leftover rice fried up with kimchi
	Wednesday	Mandu Guk - Dumpling soup
	Thursday	Dak Bulgogi - Spicy marinated chicken
	Friday	Jjajangmyeon - Black bean noodles
	Saturday	Bossam - Boiled pork with ssam (lettuce wrap) fixings
week 3	Sunday	Galbitang - Short rib soup
	Monday	Miyeok Guk - Seaweed soup
	Tuesday	Galbi - Grilled short ribs
	Wednesday	Kimbap - Seaweed rice rolls
	Thursday	Dak Bulgogi - Spicy marinated chicken
	Friday	Dolsot Bibimbap - Stone pot rice bow
	Saturday	Yangnyeom Tongdak - Fried chicken drumsticks in spicy sauce

Expanded guide on balancing the five taste profiles in Korean cuisine, based on the recipes in this cookbook:

Sweetness

- Use brown rice syrup, honey, Korean red beans (pat), or Asian pears to add sweetness to sauces and marinades. Brown rice syrup contributes mild sweetness and viscosity.
- Garnish bibimbap with fruits like pineapple or honeydew melon. The juicy sweetness balances the other flavors.
- Add sweet potatoes or corn to vegetable dishes. They have a subtle sweetness that complements the umami.

Spiciness

- Incorporate gochujang (Korean red pepper paste) into sauces, stews, and soups. It provides a rich, fermented spiciness.
- Sprinkle gochugaru (Korean red pepper flakes) when sautéing meats or vegetables. Use it sparingly so the spice doesn't overwhelm.
- Add fresh chili peppers or kimchi to dishes for a bright, fresh heat. Adjust the amount to your taste.

Salty

- Always marinate meats and fish in soy sauce and salt. Soy sauce adds a savory saltiness.
- Use doenjang (fermented soybean paste) in soups and stews. A little goes a long way in providing a salty, funky flavor.
- Add seaweed like miyeok to soups. It gives a mineral saltiness and ocean flavor.

Sourness

- Add rice vinegar to marinades, salads, and soups. It has a mild tang that brightens other flavors.
- Use lemon or lime juice to season meats, fish, or vegetables. The acidity cuts through richness.
- Incorporate kimchi into soups and stews. The fermented sourness balances the seasoning.

Umami

- Use soy sauce to boost the umami flavors of dishes. A splash enhances meatiness.
- Add seaweed and mushrooms. They are rich in savory glutamates.
- Marinate meat in an Asian pear or apple sauce. The fruit enzymes heighten umami.
- Include mollusks like octopus or squid for an umami boost in seafood dishes.

By skillfully balancing these 5 taste profiles, you can achieve the complex and addictive flavors that define authentic Korean cuisine.

With a mix of weekday meals and weekend recipes, you can enjoy the best of Korean cuisine!

SOME TIPS FOR SUBSTITUTIONS AND ADAPTATIONS WHEN YOU CAN'T FIND TRADITIONAL KOREAN INGREDIENTS, BASED ON THE RECIPES IN THIS COOKBOOK:

Substitutions for Korean Ingredients

- If you can't find gochujang (Korean red pepper paste), you can substitute a blend of sriracha and miso paste. Start with a 3:1 ratio and adjust to taste.
- For doenjang (Korean fermented soybean paste), use an equal amount of Japanese miso paste. They have a similar salty, fermented flavor.
- If you don't have rice vinegar, you can substitute with apple cider vinegar or white wine vinegar.
- Instead of using Korean radish (mu) or daikon radish, opt for regular red radishes.
- For Korean glass noodles (dangmyun), use cellophane noodles or mung bean noodles.

Adaptations for Hard-to-Find Ingredients

- If you can't find napa cabbage for kimchi, use regular green cabbage instead.
- For Asian pears, substitute regular pears. They work well for marinades.
- If you don't have jujubes (Korean red dates), try using regular dried dates.
- Instead of Korean chile peppers, use serrano or jalapeño peppers. Adjust the quantity based on heat level.
- For Korean seaweed like miyeok, kombu or wakame make good substitutes.
- If you lack sesame oil, substitute with vegetable oil and add sesame seeds.

With a combination of suiwtable substitutions and adaptations, you can still create delicious Korean dishes without access to all the traditional ingredients. Get creative with what you have on hand!

THE OTHER BOOKS OF MINE

Printed in Great Britain
by Amazon

39284144R00046